Praise for *Money-Making Mom*

"One of the most exciting trends I've noticed in the past decade is the number of at-home moms who are creating extra income by turning hobbies and passions into businesses. This is an area that's set to explode! That's why I'm so fired up that Crystal is providing hard-working moms a playbook for winning with a home business. Crystal's already made a name for herself doing this, and now it's your turn!"

—Dave Ramsey, *New York Times* bestselling author and nationally syndicated radio show host

"Crystal is a breath of fresh air in the money-advice space—she's honest and inspiring in the most relatable way. Our readers and I are always eager to hear what she has to say."

—Sarah Smith, executive editor, *Redbook*

"Is there something special you are saving for: a home project, a trip with the kids, or new piece of furniture? Do you find that if you could make some extra money, the monthly bill paying would be less stressful? Are you looking for a way to use your natural skills and talents to serve the needs of others or to fund the own needs of your family from your home? If this is your dream, Crystal Paine gives you all the practical steps to make this dream a reality for you in *Money-Making Mom*. Follow her fabulous advice and you will soon be planning how to best steward your extra cash!"

—Dee Ann Turner, vice president of corporate talent, Chick-fil-A, Inc., and author, *It's My Pleasure: The Impact of Extraordinary Talent and a Compelling Culture*

"There's got to be more than getting by with less, right? We all know it. But some of us feel trapped by our finances and don't know how to move forward. Thankfully, Crystal Paine's new book, *Money-Making Mom*, reveals how to climb out of the hole so we can start using our wealth to benefit others."

—Michael Hyatt, *New York Times* bestselling author, *Platform*, and blogger, MichaelHyatt.com

"Thank you so much for the opportunity to read this book! I read it in two days . . . it was so hard to put down. I closed the book with pages of ideas coupled with driving motivation! I feel empowered to use my own talents in new ways. Crystal does a marvelous job providing encouragement for women in business."

—Sarah

"*Money-Making Mom* makes me feel like I can. Crystal not only inspires me to think I can, she also helps me to do so by giving practical tips in the book about how to deal with failure and insecurity and how to move forward. She has inspired me to set a few scary goals of my own, but she also made them less scary by teaching me to break them down into bite-sized chunks."

—Cathy

"There are many things I appreciated about this book. It is a walk-you-by-the-hands book on the how, what, and why of finding your money-making ability! This book requires you to dig deep in all the best ways, to find what you really love and do what you really love. I love that it is not a 'one size fits all' or a 'do what I did' type of book. I really love that you do not come away after reading it with a burden of feeling like you have to tackle this big project monster, instead you come away empowered with a sense of clear focus and direction for where your real passions lie."

—Rachel

"Thank you so much for allowing me to get an early look at *Money-Making Mom*. I read it last week and really enjoyed it. I don't usually mark up books, but I found myself dog-earing and highlighting all over the place on this one. There were a ton of ideas in this book, and my favorite part was that none of them were quick fixes. So many self-help books want to change your life overnight, but this book encouraged women to build their businesses slowly and with intention."

—Jill

"*Money-Making Mom* holds a message every American needs to read. I rarely highlight or take notes in books. This book pulled creativity out of me that I didn't realize I had. I was able to formulate a few business ideas through the first few chapters. The whole book has my notes littered in it though. Not only were there many practical tips and examples, but the heartbeat of the book was filled with substance way beyond the normal entrepreneur. The feeling I had after finishing the book was excitement for the future, realism of the hard work ahead of me, and acceptance of who I am and how I can use my gifts."

—Mariah

"This book is just the jump-start to get creative juices flowing, the encouragement to be more successful, and the challenge to make a difference in other people's lives."

—Carrie

"Crystal Paine's new book is a perfect blend of the practical and the philosophical. It contains a wealth of actionable steps and exercises to help any woman move her business idea from inkling to existence, but it's when she addresses the 'whys' that she really shines. I've read so many business and entrepreneurial books lately, but this is the first one that's dug deeply at my heart and challenged me to consider what I'm really trying to accomplish in bringing in extra income."

—Elissa

"Crystal Paine mentors the reader every step of the journey from identifying one's skills and passions to determining one's mission in life and connecting those to a money-making venture. It's filled with practical advice about educating yourself, choosing a domain name, growing your business, and adding employees. As you read, you feel as if you're sitting with Crystal discussing your ideas over a cup of coffee. This is not a 'get rich quick' scheme; Crystal's own candor about her failures makes *Money-Making Mom* a refreshing departure from other books of this genre. Read it, and you'll be encouraged in starting your own business."

—Karen

"This book gave me some great ideas about ways to earn money, but above all, it inspired me to give back to others in need. Having this new purpose of helping others through my finances (as small as they may be) is a huge motivation to earn money. I am incredibly thankful for this book and the realization that I can make a difference in the lives of those who need it!"

—Elizabeth

"I consider myself to be well read and have an advanced degree. I was a little skeptical that there would be any new insights in this book. However, it was not only motivating but I also learned some new ways to find opportunities for income. I will definitely be putting these methods to use."

—Alice

"Crystal was so open and honest in her writing, reading it felt like she was a close friend sharing ideas and stories with me over a cup of coffee. The book not only gave me ideas for living debt-free, saving money, and earning extra income for my family, but gave me the confidence and motivation to make a difference in these ways."

—Kelly

"As a woman, who has a regular 8–5 career and doesn't have children, I found this book very enlightening and encouraging. It offers many ideas of how to earn extra income to provide for your family but more importantly it inspires all women, no matter their situation, to find their passion and live it to the fullest."

—Jessica

"At the onset of the book, I expected to be informed but not changed. Instructed but not inspired. Well, I was wrong! From Chapter 2 on, the story was no longer Crystal's, it was mine. I pondered what makes me uniquely gifted to serve others while earning money. What dreams do I have that could be reached if I were able to contribute to my family's income-earning potential? What could I do that would minimally disrupt my ability to be a stay at home, homeschooling mom? Around Chapter 4, I began considering a consulting business. At Crystal's prompting in Chapter 3, I began researching and polled a few friends who might like to use my services only to find that I was immediately overwhelmed and underprepared for what would be required to execute the plan. Not to worry. Crystal addresses failure in the book! It's all part of the process.

I continued to reexamine my question from above: 'what makes me uniquely gifted to serve others while earning money?' One night, just before bed, it came to me! An epiphany. I launched into a business idea that seemed so easy and so obvious, I couldn't believe that I hadn't thought of it before."

—Robin

"I have been an avid reader of Crystal Paine's writing since the very early days of her mommy blog and have enjoyed watching the evolution of her personal growth and writing style through the years. In my opinion, *Money-Making Mom* is her best work yet! Very informative, detailed, and full of not only Crystal's experiences in business, but also the experiences of other moms, this book is a must-have for those looking for ways to make money. No matter what stage of life you are in, if you have the desire to start a business, Crystal's encouragement and guidance are certain to help you succeed!"

—Stephanie

"This is the best book I've read on making money from home. I like the fact that this book is not about getting rich quick. Not only is this book about making money from home, but this book is about finding out what your passions and skills are, how to grow your business at a steady pace, work life balance and generosity. I love that Crystal uses real life examples of real people from all walks of life. This book isn't just for stay-home moms but for every mom."

—Lisa

"In the last three years, I don't think I've missed a single post on MoneySavingMom.com. In fact, I've been an avid reader, often even reading old posts, and I honestly thought that there couldn't be much new that Crystal could tell me. I mean, I've been following her for years now. And yet, after the first chapter of *Money-Making Mom*, I was surprised to find that thus far, I had just barely tapped the wealth of her knowledge and experience. This book was brimming with great advice, wisdom, and guidance.

Unlike many other money-making books, this one marches to the beat of a different drummer. Rather than simply storing up treasures for ourselves, Crystal recognizes the true beauty of success in serving others and is continually reminding us to make an impact and give generously. It was so encouraging to me to read that I have something to give to the world, a way to make the world better for others. I really appreciated that element of *Money-Making Mom*."

—Deana

"*Money-Making Mom* is for those who have taken their monthly budget down to the bare bones and still find there is not enough income. This book invites you to think outside the box and encourages you to look at how you can use your talents and passions to help contribute to your family's income. I enjoyed reading the ideas and strategies to help make my goals a reality. I felt the step-by-step questions were insightful and helped me to stop and think about what I truly care about. And while we all want more wiggle room in our family budget, the ultimate goal for this book is to help families financially so they can be generous and give more to the charities or organizations they truly want to support."

—Nicole

MONEY-MAKING MOM

How Every Woman Can Earn More and Make a Difference

CRYSTAL PAINE

NELSON
BOOKS

An Imprint of Thomas Nelson

Published in Nashville, Tennessee, by Nelson Books, an imprint of Thomas Nelson. Nelson Books and Thomas Nelson are registered trademarks of HarperCollins Christian Publishing, Inc.

Author is represented by Esther Fedorkevich, c/o The Fedd Agency, Inc., Literary Agency, P.O. Box 341973, Austin, TX 78734.

Thomas Nelson titles may be purchased in bulk for educational, business, fundraising, or sales promotional use. For information, please e-mail SpecialMarkets@ ThomasNelson.com.

Any Internet addresses, phone numbers, or company or product information printed in this book are offered as a resource and are not intended in any way to be or to imply an endorsement by Thomas Nelson, nor does Thomas Nelson vouch for the existence, content, or services of these sites, phone numbers, companies, or products beyond the life of this book.

Some names and identifying details have been changed to protect the privacy of individuals.

ISBN: 978-1-4002-0649-0 (eBook)
ISBN: 978-0-7180-8854-5 (TP)

Library of Congress Control Number: 2015939915

ISBN: 978-1-4002-0648-3

Printed in the United States of America

16 17 18 19 20 RRD 6 5 4 3 2 1

Contents

Introduction

ASHLEY SITS AT THE KITCHEN TABLE, STEAMING CUP OF coffee in her hand, staring into blank space to avoid the stack of collection notices on the table. But the pile looms regardless, along with the nagging whispers of an ever-dwindling bank account balance. As her kids sleep soundly in the next room, Ashley anxiously wonders what she can possibly do to fix these harsh financial realities and avoid what is likely a teetering future for her family.

Though Ashley is a fictitious person, her situation is not unique. Perhaps you can relate. Many people today feel strapped—living paycheck to paycheck, suffocated by student loans or credit card debt, and wondering how on earth they're going to round up the money needed for this month's basic living expenses. I've read countless e-mails and blog comments about the financial struggles many families face, and I can nod in empathy. While I can't, of course, personally relate to all of their financial situations, I do know what it's like to feel trapped by limited income and desperate, trying to figure out ways to get (and save) more money.

And that's just one reason this book is dear to my heart. I'm stoked to share the important lessons (through many tries, failures, and ultimate successes) that helped carve out my family's path to financial freedom. Hopefully I'll be able to save you from repeating the same mistakes I made!

I wrote this book to teach women how to increase their incomes and use it to make an impact, while at the same time maintaining a healthy balance of priorities. Whether you are feeling the stress that comes from an unexpected financial crisis or looking for a little extra side income or are the primary breadwinner in your family, these pages will empower you with practical ideas for starting a business or finding a creative way to make a part- or full-time income. In addition they will provoke you to think about making a difference with that income—whether to help your family get in a better financial position or to give generously to a cause you're passionate about.

Regardless if you are married, single, have children or don't, live on a one- or two-income budget, I want to inspire and encourage you to:

- stop living under the stress of barely making it
- stop feeling desperate and discouraged when you look at your bank statements
- stop worrying about an uncertain financial tomorrow
- stop living without intention

Through the lessons learned and wisdom cultivated from my journey and those of many other women from all walks of life, I want to challenge and help you to:

- find the freedom to dream big and set long-term financial goals

- start thinking creatively
- forge an intentional pathway for your future in line with your priorities
- best of all: be in a position to help others along the way

I will show you, through real-life examples, that no matter how bad of a financial situation you may feel you're in right now, you're not stuck. Or trapped. I want to help you find a way to start over in a new direction.

Entrepreneurialism is something I've always been passionate about. I love helping people find creative ways to earn more money. And I've learned how important it is to keep a balanced perspective. The reality is . . .

Money doesn't buy happiness.
Money doesn't equal fulfillment.
Money doesn't solve your emotional problems.
Money doesn't give you purpose.

If it did, the richest people in this world would be some of the happiest, most emotionally healthy people in existence. In reality, many of them are struggling through divorce, depression, and addictions, just like many people who don't make a seven-figure annual salary.

Properly stewarded, money can be an amazing tool and a resource for those who need it not only to survive but to live with purpose. It can help feed and clothe the hungry. It can build houses, schools, and hospitals in the poorest of countries. It can provide nourishment and medicine for malnourished children. It can help your disabled neighbor pay her rent or help you buy groceries for your recently widowed aunt.

For the past few years, my husband, Jesse, and I have used some of the proceeds of my book sales and blog earnings to fund a Child Survival Program with Compassion International for 130 to 160 moms and babies in the Dominican Republic. This wonderful organization provides food, medical care, education, marketable skills training, and spiritual mentoring to mothers and babies living in poverty. We had the opportunity to visit the Dominican Republic in 2012 to see this program at work. We were forever changed and moved at a deep soul level to continue to help however we can.

I realize that there are many pressing needs around the world. None of us can obliterate worldwide poverty, but if each of us wisely stewards our finances so that we can give generously, we can collectively have a powerful impact in reaching those who are in need.

Financial freedom has a lot to do with cultivating a deeper perspective of life, a shift in priorities, and a greater significance in your purpose than you may have ever thought about.

However different (and hopefully better!) your life, your bank statements, your financial goals, and your business plans look weeks, months, or even years after reading this book, remember: Use your resources wisely. Invest your time carefully. And make the most of what you have been given so that you can bless others generously. Because that's a big part of what life is all about.

I'm excited as you step out into a great adventure, not only learning strategies to generate more income, but also finding meaning and purpose as you do it.

1

First Steps to Financial Freedom

*Many people make the mistake of thinking that all
the challenges in their lives would dissipate if they just
had enough money. Nothing could be further from
the truth. Earning more money, in and of itself, rarely
frees people. It's equally ridiculous to tell yourself that
greater financial freedom and mastery of your finances
would not offer you greater opportunities to expand,
share, and create value for yourself and others.*

—ANTHONY ROBBINS

THE SOUND WAS DEAFENING. RAIN PELTED DOWN, LIGHTning bolts flashed, thunder crashed in rapid succession, while the wind howled and rocked our flimsy aluminum trailer. My tenyear-old little self huddled in a damp corner. All around me were varying-sized pots and pails on the verge of overflowing with rainwater leaking through the ceiling and windows.

This hailstorm was the product of two separate thunderstorms that hit within hours of each other in the Wichita, Kansas, area. It is also on record as one of the worst storms in the history of the state. Experiencing this was definitely scary. Waiting out the torrential weather in the flabby construction trailer where we were living was a whole other level of frightening. But this was just par for the financial course my parents were charting.

And I am so grateful.

Yes, you read that right. I said I was grateful to have gone through such a terrifying hailstorm without a sturdy basement to take shelter in. Well, okay, so I'm not sure I'm thankful for the storm itself, but I am so thankful that my parents decided to make sacrifices and live their lives counter-culturally as far as money management is concerned.

Mom and Dad's frugal lifestyle and wise financial choices weren't something they learned entirely on their own; these lessons were handed down to them by their parents. One thing Pop (my dad's dad) ingrained in my father was that you should never go into debt for anything except a house. From the beginning of my parents' marriage, they followed this principle.

When I was around six years old, my parents made a radical decision to work hard and sacrifice in order to pay off the mortgage on our house. They were frugal, spending their money wisely and setting aside every bit of extra cash from raises or bonuses to pay off the mortgage. My mom never bought new clothes; instead, she either made them or we shopped at thrift stores. She also gave us haircuts, baked our bread, bought in bulk, and always looked for ways to get the best deal on any purchase she needed to make. My dad took care of repairs around the house and on our vehicles. If he didn't know how to do something, he usually figured it out on his own (my dad is a very smart and handy man). We used what we had, wore a lot of hand-me-downs, drove used cars, and learned a lot about contentment in the process.

I still remember how exciting it was when my parents' hard work came to fruition and they paid off our house. The relief and fulfillment of not having a mortgage was something that I could feel even as a young child. Soon after, my parents took their financial ambition to the next level. They had dreamt of building a house, debt-free, out in the country. So they began saving every dime and thinking up creative ways to make their dream a reality.

Four years later, Mom and Dad found the perfect plot of land. They purchased it with much of their savings and sold our paid-for house. This was all well and good except for the looming question of where we would live while they built our new house. My dad quickly provided the solution to that equation when he rented a single-wide construction trailer from the real estate development company where he worked. Yes, the very same trailer I talked about in the beginning of this chapter.

The minute the big semitruck pulled that trailer into the newly poured gravel driveway on our just-purchased property, the adventure began. Our first matter of business was to secure the trailer propped up on cement blocks to the ground as tightly as possible using cables and stakes. Then, it was time to clean. Every inch of the trailer needed elbow grease. There was dirt and filth everywhere we looked, from the stained, deep blue-carpeted floor to the grimy cheap wood paneling to the cobweb-covered ceiling.

After spending days deep in bleach, the seven of us got the trailer into livable shape, moved most of our possessions into a storage unit, and moved the basic necessities into that trailer. For the first few days, it felt like we were on vacation in a rustic cabin. But that euphoria quickly wore off.

Our temporary home didn't have an oven, air-conditioning, or heat. It also didn't have a regular door, but rather a glass storefront one that offered little privacy and little protection against the hot Kansas summer sun and the unusually cold autumn that year. The trailer also leaked every time it rained. We endured many torrential storms that summer, battling legitimate fears of flooding by scattering kitchen pots and pans under the leaky ceiling and stuffing rolled-up bath towels in the sopping windows. Since we only had space for a washing machine, we had planned to line dry all our laundry. However, the frequent rain prevented us from hanging our laundry to dry outside much of the time. Instead, it required many treks to the laundromat and many hours hanging out there while we waited for our loads of laundry to dry.

Without an oven, we befriended a myriad of other kitchen appliances, learning how to bake birthday cakes in the microwave and create dozens of different meals in the electric skillet and slow cooker. Without air-conditioning, the dry Kansas heat felt unbearable some days. We would take cold showers or hog the space directly in front of the fan to get some relief. When autumn arrived, temperatures took a dive. For the first time in years, it snowed in October. We traded our lament of the suffocating heat for fears of frostbite, snuggling under endless layers of sweaters and articles of clothing, because all of our coats and most of our winter blankets were in storage.

Did I mention the bad mice problem? We had seen some pesky rodents darting around when we first started cleaning the trailer, but we assumed a good cleaning would get rid of them. Not so much! We often woke up to find mice droppings in our kitchen or yet another item that had been chewed up and destroyed in the middle of the night by the furry pests.

Despite the inconveniences, we truly have so many happy memories of that time in our lives. And, looking back, I would not trade the experience for the world. We celebrated when we moved into our new house, not only because we finally had a house with the many conveniences we had missed, but because my parents had fulfilled their dream of building a house debt-free.

Let me tell you, Pop's encouragement to my dad to never go into debt except for a house and then seeing my parents take that advice and go even further with it powerfully impacted me for life—especially seeing how the absence of a monthly house payment afforded financial room for my parents to give generously. I have always admired them for anonymously helping so many different people. I can't tell you how many times they have donated finances and supplies not only to those in their local church but also to missionaries around the world and to families in need in their own neighborhood.

What Mom and Dad offered me as a child and into my adult years as my husband Jesse and I started a family of our own was a healthy picture of financial freedom—in living and giving. Truly, my husband and I owe so much to our parents and grandparents. I know beyond any shadow of a doubt that we would never be in the position we are financially, nor would we have paid cash for our first house, were it not for their influence and examples. We are eternally grateful!

The Power of Financial Freedom

The words *financial freedom* bring to mind different things for different people. I asked my readers to weigh in on what these words mean to them, and I would like to share some of their thoughts.

(To me) financial freedom means:

- being able to provide for my family without stressing over whether or not I'm going to be able to make ends meet from month to month
- not having to worry about which bills to pay this month, how we'll have money to buy groceries, where we'll get the funds to pay for gas to get to work, etc. It would mean actually having a savings account, and being able to pay off debt.
- having enough for what we need with a little left over for what we want

Other definitions included the following:

- being debt-free
- having x amount of savings
- building a retirement fund
- paying off looming medical bills
- building a college fund for one's children

These are great responses, but, to me, financial freedom is about more than just a bigger paycheck, a better nest egg, or a less stressful existence. I love what one of my readers, Megan, said: "Increasing our income has allowed us to breathe easier and live, save, and give exactly how we want to." She shared her story of how she was able to create financial freedom in her own life. I'd like to pass on her inspiring words to you.

I'm a special education teacher by training and for six years worked as a preschool teacher for children with hearing loss. When my husband and I found out that we were expecting our first child we wanted to find a way for me to stay at home while still making a part-time income. We are committed to living debt-free and knew I would have to make at least some money, even with a pared down budget, to keep that commitment.

I worked out a deal to work one day a week doing at-home visits through my school but this currently only gives me about three to four hours per week. I started searching online to see what else I could do from home and I began doing a little mystery shopping. While this wasn't ideal (I couldn't bring my son along to many of the shops), it helped bring in a little more money.

I then stumbled upon the idea of online selling. I currently sell on Amazon using the Fulfillment by Amazon program and I LOVE it! I buy inventory through a mix of retail arbitrage, thrifting, and wholesale and send it directly to Amazon's warehouse. They store it, ship it when it sells, and I collect my money. I can work as little or as much as I want, I can bring my son along sourcing with me, and I'm making more than I ever thought I could while working in my yoga pants at home. I'm slowly figuring this "working mom" thing out, but this has allowed me to still contribute to the family finances so we can continue to live within our means and be able to give to our church.

Did you catch Megan's last statement? The hard effort she put in not only gave her family breathing room in their budget but also allowed them to be able to give more.

This, my friends, is the heartbeat of financial freedom. It's being in the place where you can be intentional with your money. Where you're not constantly living paycheck to paycheck, trying to survive, trying to make ends meet, hoping that you're going to be able to pay all of your bills this month. It's being able to plan ahead, save ahead, and give generously.

My hope for this book is to give you inspiration, encouragement, and practical ideas so that you can experience this kind of financial freedom. So that you no longer live under the stress of "barely making it." So that you no longer feel desperate and discouraged when you look at your bank statements. So that you can begin to live on less than you make and be in a position to help others.

Free to Make Changes

Those last few paragraphs might sound unrealistic and pie-in-the-sky for some of you. But I truly believe this kind of financial freedom is possible and attainable for everyone reading this book who is willing to work hard, set goals, think creatively, make sacrifices, and, most importantly, not give up.

Why do I believe this? Because I have experienced it. From the time Jesse and I were married, we had established goals for our family including living debt-free and having residual income to supplement Jesse's paycheck. Most important was our vision to live on less than we make so we could give more. We longed to be able to live out one of our family mottos: "Live simply so that others can simply live."

At first, our big goals seemed more like unrealistic dreams, considering that for the first few years of our marriage, we were barely scraping by on our part-time incomes. In fact, as I chronicled in my book *Say Goodbye to Survival Mode*, during those years we often made less than $1,000 each month.

In order to stay debt-free and be in a position to live out our vision, we spent many years pinching pennies; buying only necessities; waiting to make purchases until we could pay for them with cash; carefully monitoring our spending habits; living on a strict, written budget; having many heart-to-heart (and sometimes hard) conversations to stay on the same page with our finances as a couple; trying many different ways to generate extra income (many that flopped, as I'll share later in this book!); and ultimately creating a solid income from MoneySavingMom.com. It wasn't easy, but with much dedication, goal setting, hard work, and time, we set out on our unique path to financial freedom.

Only a few months before I started writing this book, our family finally made the decision to move from Wichita, Kansas, to Nashville, Tennessee. The move was about three years in the making and was much prayed, thought, talked, mulled, cried, and counseled over. It was a big change and not an easy one to make. It meant saying good-bye to family and friends near and dear to our hearts. It meant moving out of our geographic comfort zone and everything we had known for all of our lives. (Up until 2014, I had never lived outside of the state of Kansas!) It meant making adjustments to a new house, a new city, and a new state.

There are many reasons we made this major leap, but I can sum them up in one word: *change.*

Jesse needed a change. In the past year, the light had gone out in my husband's eyes. So had the passion from his heart, the spring in his step. He started his law firm in 2008. It was exciting to see him turn a dream into a reality and help many, many people. While he was grateful for the opportunity, running the demanding law firm had taken its toll, and he was ready for something different. The time had come to move on. Jesse wanted to pursue some legal/business ideas that had been patiently waiting on the back burner. Additionally, he was considering taking on a managerial role in MoneySavingMom.com.

Our family also needed a change. We loved being close to family in Kansas. We loved being able to see them often, spend time with them, and build close relationships with them. And we miss them dearly. But Jesse and I both running separate businesses was beginning to wear on us. We didn't have as much margin as we wanted for doing life together as a family. We longed for a slower pace of life and more community.

Finally, our business needed a change. MoneySavingMom.com has grown a lot in the past few years. While we were grateful for the growth and excited at the possibilities and open doors, it had become much more than I could handle on my own. So in 2013 we hired a wonderful management company to help shoulder a tremendous amount of the load I had been carrying. Moving to Nashville, where our management company is located, allowed for more efficiency when it came to having team meetings, developing products, and increasing business growth versus trying to do all these things long-distance.

Having a much more flexible schedule since Jesse is working from home instead of running a busy law firm has been a welcome, and much needed, change for us. We love being home as a family more. We love having Jesse more involved in our everyday lives. And we love a simpler pace of life where relationships are much more important than productivity and to-do lists.

The only reason our family was able to say yes to making these considerable yet needed changes was because we constructed and set in place a solid plan to create financial freedom. We invested years of time and effort, established strong sources of income outside of a traditional 8:00 A.M. through 5:00 P.M. job, and were then able to step back and ask, "What do we want our life to look like in the future?"

Realizing that we were in a place to choose to downsize our businesses and simplify our lives was a beautiful thing. We didn't have to keep chasing after more—more business, more money, or more fulfillment. The financial foundation we had in place gave us true freedom to make choices that were in the best interest of our marriage, our children, and our long-term goals.

Creating Your Vision

In a minute, I'm going to ask you to pause, reflect, and capture your vision on paper. But first, I want to talk about what financial freedom is *not*, to help bring more clarity to your personal genesis of breathing easier.

Financial freedom is not:

- something so overwhelming that only women with superpowers and amazing organizational skills can obtain it
- getting rich quickly
- working sixteen-hour days and burning out as a result
- building the biggest business or making as much money as possible
- using other people in order to catapult your own success
- sacrificing for an idea or a new business at the cost of not seeing or spending quality time with your loved ones
- having more money just to have more money

Financial freedom is:

- making choices based upon what is best for you and your family and that align with your long-term goals
- thinking big and creatively
- using the skills and talents you were born with
- taking calculated risks and trying new things
- turning knowledge and available resources into income-generating ideas
- being in a position to give generously
- using your time and talents to bless others and make an impact

I want you to take some time to stop and consider where you are right now and what financial freedom might look like for you.

Maybe you are a single mom and juggling three jobs for chump change is simply not cutting it. Maybe you're a stay-at-home mom whose husband just got laid off, and you need some cash to get through this hard time. Maybe you are just sick and tired of punching in at 8:00 A.M. and leaving at 5:00 P.M. at a lackluster job that leaves you unmotivated and unfulfilled. Maybe you're tired of scrambling to find money to pay your mortgage, rent, car payment, or electric bill. Maybe you are tired of having to borrow money from your parents or close friends. Maybe you want to have more wiggle room in your budget. Maybe you want to start saying yes to help feed the homeless in your community, buy groceries for the widow down the block, or provide clean water for a child in a third world country for a year.

What does financial freedom mean to you?

Think about it. I mean, *really* think about it.

Don't let this question slip by without taking the time to answer it with deep conviction. You may need a few minutes to reflect, or you may have had the answer before you started reading this chapter. Write down your thoughts in the space below. This is the vision, *your* vision, that I will be helping you achieve as you read through this book.

_____

_____

_____

_____

Switch to New Thinking

Financial freedom is not just about getting your finances in order. It's about mentally getting your head in the right space.

You have to believe that you can stand on your own two feet and live in financial freedom. You have to believe that there are options out there that will work, regardless of your particular season of life or unique circumstance. You have to believe in your vision then make positive changes that help propel you and that vision forward. (Throughout this book, I'll show you how!)

I am not going to lie to you. Creating financial freedom takes work, practice, sweat, and tears. There will be many struggles and disappointments along the way. Just as a baby will never learn how to walk if he gives up halfway through the process, you will never realize financial success if you quit.

And don't just think that living out financial freedom means getting a higher-paying job. I can't tell you how many e-mails I receive from people who say they wish they could be in our financial position but it's just not possible because they only make $25,000 per year. Truth be told, not too long ago, making $25,000 per year would have been a significant pay increase for us as we were barely making it on $600 to $1,000 per month!

When you see what is possible, you begin to understand that there is no "one" way or "right" way to get there. You can begin—yes, even right now!—to exhale knowing there are so many different opportunities to build income, many of which I will talk about throughout this book. I have learned much over the past ten years (and counting!) of this journey of entrepreneurial endeavors and failures. And so have the wonderful women I've met along the way, some of whose stories I'll also share with you in the coming pages.

2

What Makes You You

We are not in a position in which we
have nothing to work with.
We already have capacities, talents,
direction, missions, callings.

—ABRAHAM MASLOW

I SAT IN BED AS MY STOMACH CHURNED. THE MERE thought of a saltine cracker made me queasy. I tried to get comfortable, which is not an easy feat when you have a burgeoning belly and you're surrounded by a chaotic mess of laptop and legal pads and journals scribbled with ideas from brainstorming sessions. Disheartened and distraught, I stared at the computer screen and sighed.

My husband was in law school when we found out I was pregnant with our first baby. I was extremely sick for the first five months and had to quit my job as a mother's helper. While I wanted to be a stay-at-home mom, I knew there was no way we could live on my husband's income alone. However, I could not for the life of me come up with anything I could do to earn money from home. I was good at a lot of different things but didn't feel I had one particular outstanding talent or exceptional know-how that I could turn into profit.

In the past, I'd had a lot of different side jobs, but none of them was conducive for doing from home—especially when I had a baby to care for. I remember how desperate I felt, spending hours and hours online each week searching for an idea that didn't require any start-up cash. I knew I had to figure this out quickly. Our bills were piling up faster than money was coming in. But all this brain wracking, Google searching, and entrepreneurial–book reading resulted in nothing but more discouragement. Maybe I just wasn't cut out to have an at-home business. Frantic, I got on my knees and begged God for ideas.

I cannot tell you how many times over the course of my life, in person and on my blog, people tell me they don't have a clue what they are good at or what they could even do to earn money. Maybe you get this feeling. Maybe you're shaking your head asking, "Crystal, is it really possible for me to find a way to earn an income? I mean, I know other people have been successful at it, but they're different. They have gifts, talents, abilities. And me? Well, I've got nothing."

I think about the hundreds of e-mails and comments I receive from women expressing this same sentiment. Tara, a mom of three young girls, wrote:

> I don't think I can do or make anything that people would pay money for. I'm not artsy-craftsy. The idea of being a saleswoman is repulsive to me. I've thought about selling deodorant or lotion, or trying my hand at soap-making, but it seems like the natural toiletries market is pretty small around here (Montgomery, AL) and Etsy is flooded with these kinds of products already. And

they're so easy and inexpensive to make at home, I don't know why anyone wouldn't!

Often, people will assume that my success as a blogger came from an immediate instinctual clue that writing and online marketing were my "things." In reality, that could not be further from the truth. I didn't know what my "thing" was and had to stumble along, experiment a lot, and make many mistakes before I uncovered my gifts.

Looking back, I realize that as a child, I loved to read. I loved writing stories. I loved writing in my dozens of journals. And I loved writing to my ever-growing list of pen pals. (At one point, I think I simultaneously corresponded with sixty or more people from all over the country, many of whom I wrote to at least once every other month!)

I was also fascinated by computers at an early age, years before I even knew about the existence of the Internet, which didn't become such a big deal until I was a teenager. When I was about fourteen, I bought a used computer and set it up in my bedroom. I spent hours writing articles and designing graphics for a small newsletter I published for young girls, working on my rudimentary website that a friend had built for me, learning more about building websites, running an online message board, and answering e-mails.

It's clear to me now that what I'm doing today is the perfect union of the passions and interests I have had since I was young. But it took me years to be able to see that.

The Discovery Process

If you feel inexperienced, unmarketable, or unskilled, know that you are not alone. I talk to so many women who feel as though they just don't have much to offer to the world. They feel so average and untalented compared to many other women.

But here's the thing: I strongly believe that every person has unique giftings and abilities. Those things might not be obvious to you and, like I experienced, they may take some effort and experimentation to fully discover, but you do have something to offer to the world, something that could turn into a viable income stream.

And today, I'm going to help you start the process of digging deep and excavating that buried talent and treasure. Because there is only one you, and the world needs what you have to offer.

To help you answer the question of, "What am I good at that can generate income?" let's explore your skills and talents, as well as your passions and knowledge.

Skills and Talents

A *skill* is something that anyone can learn if you study, work hard, and practice. Whereas a *talent* is something that you are naturally good at and if you invest time and effort into this area, you could potentially become amazing at it.

Both skills and talents are things that can be nurtured and improved upon and there is often overlap or correlation between the two. For instance, most athletes have some natural talent—they may have a body well built for swimming or have a strong torso or be a fast runner. By investing time to exercise, practice, and hone their natural abilities and talents, they can become even more skilled and competent in their sport.

Can you play an instrument well? Do you have a natural ability to sell? Do you have an eye for interior design? Do you have a knack for giving presentations in front of large groups of people? Do you love crunching numbers? Can you easily identify solutions to problems?

Think through what skills and talents you have. Ask your friends and family members for their input too. To get the wheels of your brain turning, here is a list of some possible skills and talents you may have:

Public speaking	Leadership
Technical writing	Problem-solving
Computers/electronics	Sales
Graphic design advertising	Athletics
Communication	Programming
Sewing	Cooking
Content marketing	Photography
Hospitality	Administration
Web design	Marketing
Networking	Singing
Accounting	Planning
Research	Systems management

Bethany has a natural talent for cooking, and she found a way to take that talent and make a small side income from it. A bachelor friend of hers, who couldn't cook to save his life, asked her if she would be willing to cook for him, adding he would pay her for the ingredients, supplies, and a flat rate for each cooked meal. Bethany said yes and every Sunday for a few months delivered to him a week's worth of meals. It was a win-win situation. This man saved money by eating at home, and Bethany made money by preparing his food. What a great idea!

Wendy, one of my blog readers, turned her graphic design skills into a side job that works with her schedule and has helped to pay down debt, build an emergency fund, and save toward special home projects. She writes,

Before I had my first child, I worked for a small advertising firm. I used my degree in graphic design to create brochures and help design different styles of blogs and company websites. I loved this work, but my husband and I had decided it was important for me to stay home with our baby when she was born.

We weren't sure how the finances would work out, reduced to just one income, but because I had a difficult pregnancy, I didn't have much time to research other options.

Finally, after I got into a rhythm with my new baby girl, I realized that at least a part-time income would be helpful to continue paying down our debt and create the emergency fund we'd always wanted, but never created.

Around that same time, our church was launching a capital campaign for a new campus, and they asked the congregation if anyone would be willing to work part-time to help with the campaign materials. I talked with our executive pastor, and was thrilled to be hired!

I began working about ten hours a week, from my computer at home. Since my baby was taking two naps a day, plus going to bed by 7:00 P.M. at night, it turned out to be quite simple to fit in that amount of work. That was seven years ago, and since then my husband and I have been blessed with two more children. I continue to work from home for our church in different capacities, using my graphic design background. We decided that all my income from church would go toward the emergency fund and then to pay off our van loan. Now that those two goals have been met, we are saving up to finish our basement.

Those of you who know me well, know that decorating is not a skill I was born with. While this is not something I have any interest in developing, I do love a well-decorated home. I have realized, however, that I can't make that happen on my own. I need the help of those skilled in the art of decorating and design.

Since our move to Tennessee, a large pile of wall art cluttered the floor of my closet, taunting me. Every time I looked at those decorative pieces, I was reminded of the fact that the walls in my home were unattractively bare. But the thought of trying to figure out where and how to arrange them is a surefire way for a non-decorator like me to break out into a sweat and experience heart palpitations. I wouldn't even know where to start. And that is exactly why the pile just sat there collecting dust and taking up space.

A few months after our move, a sweet friend of mine offered to come over and put up the wall art. Within a few hours, she and her kind husband had masterfully arranged the pile of frames on our walls. They did a phenomenal job! And I cannot tell you how refreshing it is to stare at an artful space instead of a blank wall.

It's clear to see my friend has a knack for decorating. She is in a completely different field of work, but if she had the desire, she could probably earn good money turning her skill into a business or a side business.

I realized she had this skill when she came with me to help me at a conference I was speaking at. I watched how she set up our booth so beautifully, I saw how she just loved making things look so organized and eye pleasing, and I asked her if she liked decorating. Without missing a beat, she said, "I love decorating!"

We got to talking, and I told her about my poor, empty walls and how it scared me to think of nailing something to them. Her eyes lit up and she said, "Could I please come over and help you decorate? I would be so, so happy to help you out."

I could clearly tell that she was gifted in this area—just as others could see that I had a love for computers and a gift for writing. Sometimes, it takes others seeing our gifts and pointing them out for us to really be able to identify and own those gifts.

Here are a few questions for you to consider and ask your friends for input as you consider your skills and talents:

1. What do friends and family ask you for help with?
2. What are the things that are easy for you to do?
3. What did you do well as a child?
4. Have you taught yourself how to do something because you were frustrated with the job someone else did when you hired him or her to do it?
5. Can you operate a particular piece of equipment or tool, or do you have specialized training or experience in certain areas?
6. Are there natural talents you have that, with some honing and practicing, could turn into marketable skills?

Passions and Knowledge

Think with me for a minute: What makes you come alive and feel energized? What hobbies or interests do you enjoy? Is it health, fitness, making an impact in your community, researching a specific subject, creating? Are you drawn to meeting the needs of others in your community? Do you spend hours writing and wonder where the time went? Do you love caring for animals? Things that make you feel fulfilled and excited about life are usually your *passions*.

If you want to have a successful business, it's vitally important that you have a good amount of passion for your business idea. In fact, I would encourage you to only pick an idea that you have an enormous amount of passion for. Because there are going to be many days—especially in the early stages—when the work will feel exhausting, the hours will be long, and you will need to rely heavily on your passion to keep you going.

Passion often intersects with *knowledge* because you tend to study and learn about things you are passionate about. If a subject interests you and it's something you love, you're often going to devote a lot of time to learn all you can about it.

What do you know? What are you learned in? What experience do you have in a particular subject? Are you an expert in a certain field? Knowledge is another tool you can use to increase your income. Do people ask you for help with their computer issues? Do you have medical training? Do you have experience managing personal finances?

Here are some subjects about which you may be passionate or knowledgeable:

Missions	Interior design
Health	Foreign films
Arts	Decorating
Sewing	Nature
Counseling	Fitness

Science	Business management
Education	Painting
Travel	Web video
Reading	Real estate
Childhood education	Fashion
Music	

Knowledge can also be the result of life experience. For instance, I suffered from fairly severe pregnancy-related anemia during my second pregnancy. I had to be hospitalized, have more vials of blood taken than I ever want to think about, and ultimately be induced early because I was so anemic. Because of this, I've done extensive research on the causes and cures for anemia. I wouldn't necessarily say it's a passion of mine, but out of a sheer desire to have a healthier pregnancy the third time around, I have read and studied a significant amount of information on anemia.

While it's good to think through all the areas of knowledge that you have, I encourage you to then narrow it down to those few areas that also intersect with your passions. Because, like I said above, you need passion to fuel any business endeavor. I might have a lot of knowledge about anemia, but I have zero passion for the subject. So I would never want to pursue a business related to that subject, as I'd quickly lose any interest or excitement for it.

I love how Mika turned her passion for sewing into a full-time job. Here's her story:

My business started a little something like this: I had a sewing machine I got off of Freecycle, some $1/yard fabric from Walmart, and the cheapest thread I could find. My starting expenses were literally about $10. After I learned the basics, a friend asked me to make her some rice bags. I did some research, and Froggy Girl Designs was born.

In the beginning, it was just a hobby, a way to bring in a little extra "mad money" since we had a very limited budget with four young children. After running the costs of day care, and all the other expenses related to my job at the time, my husband and I made the decision for me to stay home with them. There was still a little too much "month at the end of the money" though, so we constantly brainstormed ways to help the bottom line.

Over the last six years, what started out as a hobby has turned into a full-fledged business. That job has made up the difference many times in what a single income alone wouldn't have been able to cover. We've faced extended unemployment situations during the 2008 recession, the addition of baby number five, medical bills, broken down vehicles, and all the myriad other expenses that come up in any person's life. Froggy Girl Designs has allowed us to not be nearly as worried during those times that expenses wouldn't be met.

Currently, my profits are mostly being used toward funding my oldest son's trip to Greece and Italy with school next year, and if I can save enough, for me to accompany the trip as a chaperone. We are both *very* excited at the thought of getting to take this trip together, and through hard work and determination, I know that we'll be able to save enough for this trip without touching our standard family budget!

Amy, a mother of two young girls, is a successful ghostwriter who for thirteen years has been making a living writing. Growing up with a traditional eastern European background, she assumed she would get married at twenty and start creating a brood of children. When she was twenty-four, and still single, she realized that wasn't going to happen any time soon and decided to make other plans. While working a full-time job to pay the bills, she began using her passion to write and help others by creating press releases and articles for local companies (at first for free!). She worked hard and over time started acquiring more work and bigger projects that paid. As freelance work became more consistent, Amy quit her traditional job and began to focus on her writing passions. These assignments eventually led to writing book proposals and books for other people, some that have made it on the *New York Times* bestseller's list.

Amy told me that, as a child, she would carry a pad and pencil around everywhere she went, always thinking about and writing stories. Today, she uses her love of writing to tell powerful and life-changing stories of other people who make a difference in this world. While it took her years to build up her business, by the time she actually got married at thirty-five, she was established enough to continue working at a slower and more flexible pace when she had her children.

By the way, I am so thankful that Amy put forth all of the time and effort to hone her writing skills and develop the flourishing business she has today. She has served as a ghost editor for both my last book and the one you hold in your hands right now. She has been an incredible asset to me—saving me so much time, helping me shape book chapters and ideas with clarity, and providing such wise input and oversight into my book projects. I'm forever indebted to her!

Joy from StartAPreschool.com is a great example of someone

who turned her knowledge into residual income. She's a mom of three who started her own in-home preschool a few years ago. At the time, she was disappointed to find a lack of resources she needed to help her in the process.

After spending months testing, tweaking, and refining her ultimately successful preschool program—and making many costly mistakes along the way!—Joy determined to make it easier and less time-consuming for others hoping to do the same. She packaged the knowledge and wisdom she gained from the experience into a kit called Preschool in a Box, a comprehensive resource that helps others learn how to run a successful preschool.

This is brilliant! If Joy decided to increase her income by teaching preschool, she would have to take on more students or teach for longer hours. Instead, she used her knowledge to build a product. This onetime investment to assemble the Preschool in a Box kit has likely made her far more money than she could ever make in years of teaching preschool—and it doesn't require her to put in incredibly long hours over a long period of time.

As you consider your passions and areas of knowledge, here are some questions to help you in the discovery process:

1. What topics do you love to study or read?
2. What makes you feel excited and energetic?
3. What did you go to school for?
4. What are some areas in which your friends and family look to you as the expert?
5. What unique life experiences have you had that might equip you to counsel or help others in a way someone else might not be able to?

Ready. Set. Go!

Now that I've gotten your wheels turning and shared some inspiring stories of real-life women, I want you to do the following exercise to help you think through what type of business or income-earning idea would work for you.

The space below is divided into two sections to encourage you to reflect on your own personal skills and talents and your passions and knowledge. Start writing down whatever ideas come to your mind—big or small. If you struggle with any area, ask your spouse, best friend, or a family member for help.

Some areas may generate more ideas than others. It's okay. And if you happen to run out of space, grab a separate notebook or journal and use it to keep writing.

Finally, don't get stuck writing down only those things you feel might make you money. This is a roadblock to your subconscious. You'll likely get stuck and consequently not complete this fun and informative assignment.

So just start writing—and keep writing. Creativity breeds creativity. The more you write, the more ideas will come. Look for patterns, areas that overlap, and most importantly, ideas that especially excite you. Let this list inspire you as you contemplate moving forward with a business idea.

My Skills and Talents:

_____

_____

_____

_____

_____

_____

My Passions and Knowledge:

_____

_____

_____

_____

_____

A Formula for Success

Keep in mind, not every talent, skill, passion, or amount of knowledge you have actually will bring home the bacon. For example, your passion to ski may not earn as much income as your passion to watch other people's children. No one is going to pay you just because you speak a second language, can cook amazing dinners, love to write poems, or have a degree in communication.

Your ideal business is going to be some combination of these four areas—skills, talents, passions, and knowledge. So look for overlap in what you've written down. In addition, consider what areas you have talents and passion for and then consider what additional knowledge and skills you can learn to help turn this into a successful money-making venture.

Look through the areas and ideas you have written down and begin to brainstorm in more specific terms.

For instance:

- Can you use your passion for numbers and experience in corporate accounting to work as a part-time consultant for a local business?
- Can you use your talent and skill of writing, sewing, or cooking to host online or in-person seminars teaching others how to do the same?
- Can you use your skills and knowledge in marketing to create online courses or e-books?
- Can you use your talent speaking a different language or skills in math to tutor others?

Don't worry about hitting the nail on the head with the perfect business idea right now; I just want you to get your creative juices flowing.

Dianna, a single mom of eight-year-old twins, stumbled upon a great need in her community and ended up creating a business for it. Years ago, she bought a new dress that a local shop altered for her. The work was shoddy. In fact, the alterations were so bad, the dress didn't fit her properly and she ended up having to donate it, unworn, with tags attached, to a local charity. Frustrated at the waste of time and money, she determined to start altering her clothes herself. She did such a great job, a friend took notice and asked for her help with a dress that fit like an unflattering potato sack. She worked hard and skillfully transformed the article of clothing into a stunning, well-fitted gown. Her friend was beyond pleased with the results!

Word about the redesigned dress spread like wildfire, and more friends asked Dianna to help tailor and reshape their clothes. Inspired by the high demand for her services, she formed a partnership with multiple formal dress shops to act as a consultant for their customers. The business grew in no time.

Today, Dianna is busier than she's ever been, and she finds so much joy in making clothes that fit people well. Her love for what she does coupled with an in-demand service is helping her fund an emergency account that will cover up to six months of living expenses for her family. Fantastic!

As you consider your skills, talents, passions, and knowledge, also think about the needs that exist in your community, and even in the rest of the world, that you could help fulfill. Take a look around and figure out specific problems people face that you may be able to solve using your particular skills, talents, passions, and knowledge.

For instance, I started MoneySavingMom.com because I discovered there were so many families who wanted to decrease their grocery bills but needed practical help, ideas, and hand-holding to make it happen. I knew I had experience, knowledge, and ideas to share. I had a passion for writing and enough computer knowledge to be able to set up a blog and monetize it. I was able to marry my skills, talents, passions, and knowledge into a business that solved problems and eliminated or reduced the struggles that millions of people have.

But, as I alluded to earlier, I didn't hit on this idea from the get-go. Before I started MoneySavingMom.com, before I started blogging, and before I started writing e-books, I began my entrepreneurial adventure with a different kind of website, one that I rarely talk about because it wasn't a great idea and I have locked it up in my shame vault—you know, that secret place you bury your most embarrassing moments and really bad ideas hoping you and everyone else will forget they ever existed!

The Not-So-Perfect Formula

In 2004, when I started out reading and researching ways to make an income from home, I created a site called Covenant Wedding Source, an online business providing custom-made, modest wedding gowns and accessories. As I had personally discovered when planning my wedding, there weren't a lot of options for brides who wanted affordable wedding gowns that showed less skin. I contracted with a few exceptional seamstresses to provide the sewing services, while I focused on marketing the website and providing customers custom products made by my contractors.

My husband (always my biggest cheerleader) willingly invested $2,000 of our law school savings to start the business. That money paid for the website design, a computer, a business license, and a few other necessary supplies. I look back and wonder what got into him to willingly risk what was a huge chunk of money for my wild and crazy venture.

I had read a bunch of books from the library on starting a business, and I was pumped about my great idea. But I quickly learned I was in way over my head. I hadn't a clue about online marketing. And it didn't take long to figure out that while you can set up a great website, you need a whole lot more than that to increase your daily traffic beyond just you and your mom.

After a few weeks of very few site visits and zero sales, I became more proactive in my efforts. I joined Yahoo! Groups, left comments with a link to my site next to my name or in my bio on related online forums, wrote and submitted articles to any online site that accepted guest posts, and studied online marketing and entrepreneurialism with a vengeance. After about six months, six brides were brave enough to send in their measurements and requirements for a custom gown. Great, right? Well, I learned another lesson: creating custom-made wedding gowns according to a bride's specifications requires a massive amount of time and work to pull off—and it's especially hard to do if you are trying to do it inexpensively and from across the country!

I was discouraged to look over our bank statements and accounting ledgers and realize I had put in countless hours but had not turned a profit. This was a problem because we needed to see at least a small profit in order to survive. It was a business, after all, not a charity! Something had to change. I realized I needed to build an e-mail list, look for multiple streams of income to develop on my site, and learn more about affiliate marketing.

While I was excited to be learning new things, I was still putting in more hours than expected and seeing very little for my efforts. I started to wonder if I should discontinue the wedding business, but it was embarrassing to even think of having to admit that things hadn't worked out like I'd hoped and dreamed. I wasn't a quitter. I was determined to somehow make the business work.

Well, guess what? The next two dress projects turned out to be disasters. The customers were upset with the work, and it took weeks of pulling my hair out and brainstorming creative strategies to fix the issues and make the customers satisfied. But it was to no avail.

It was hard and humbling to admit, but it was time to close down Covenant Wedding Source. Though I initially struggled with feeling like a failure, looking back I realized what a blessing in disguise it was. Not only did I learn such valuable lessons through failure, but I also got this crazy idea to start a blog. Little did I know what those feeble blogging attempts would lead to!

Do What Works for You

I don't share this story to tell you to quit your business or idea if it's not making a ton of money in a day, week, or month. I want to encourage you to stick with an idea that will eventually provide you with a good return on your investment and that also allows you to use your gifts and skills. My wedding dress business idea wasn't a bad one; it could have worked well and been profitable for someone who could design and sew dresses herself. But because I didn't have those skills, acquired long-distance customers, and calculated my prices too low from the start, I had unknowingly structured a flawed business model that was destined to fail. No matter how much time and effort I put into it, the business would never have made much money.

An important lesson I learned was this: just because you find a need, you might not be the person to fill that need. In addition, a business idea that might work well for someone else won't necessarily work for you. When determining a business idea to pursue, focus on the areas you already excel in and that you enjoy. There is no point in spending enormous amounts of time trying to develop or hone skills you don't and won't possess.

When Kathie was in her midtwenties, she wanted to make extra cash without committing to another job and a real boss. She fell in love with Pampered Chef products at a party and signed on as a consultant. She knew a lot of people who were consultants and was impressed at the great incentives, high income, and free vacations they received. Problem was, Kathie didn't have the social skills and confidence needed to be a successful salesperson. While she was excited about the products she sold and she tried her best to network, talk to a bunch of people, and get others as hyped up as she was, she lacked that passionate zeal to keep the momentum going. Bottom line? Selling just wasn't her thing. So she bowed out of the business. Even through realizing the job wasn't a good fit, Kathie loved Pampered Chef so much that she gave it another try a few years later. But nothing had changed. She still wasn't matched well for the opportunity and ended up quitting again.

I admire Kathie's tenacity, but she gave me permission to share her story as a word of warning to others: don't invest time and money into a business idea only because it seems to work so well for others. Before jumping in, make sure that the income-earning endeavor is actually something that meshes well with your natural talents, skills, and abilities. Otherwise, there's a good chance you'll end up being miserable—and maybe even in a deeper financial hole.

When Lori was a young woman, her mother strongly encouraged her to open a jewelry shop. She writes:

I knew how to do the work but had zero experience with anything else. I did not do any research and set my prices too low; therefore, I could never make any profit and was always in the red. I was also extremely shy and couldn't stand up for myself and demand a fair price. The venture lasted about two brutal years. I finally got out, but not without owing Uncle Sam lots of money, which took me a long time to pay. I also re-discovered that I was a terrible salesperson. I was so shy and had no authority, so I would offer discounts to everyone. I ended up selling my product to another person at a loss. For now, I work in an office and I am perfectly happy there. This is where I thrive, amongst computers and paperwork, and by helping others figure out what to do. I have no interest at this time to venture out on my own.

Though Lori claimed that attempt at making money was a failure, she learned a lot from the experience. She says, "Do what you love. You will have to put tons of hours into the business and if you don't love it, it will be a nightmare. Also, don't give in to fads. Just because it's popular right now, that doesn't mean that it will still be in a couple of years."

Sometimes You Just Gotta Do What You Just Gotta Do

Some of you may be feeling a bit stressed about the concept of starting a business or doing something non-traditional to earn income. Perhaps your financial situation is pretty serious and you don't have time to brainstorm ways to make money or build on your business idea. Maybe you can't afford to waste time figuring out what you're good at and how you can make money doing it. I get it.

My heart went out to a recently divorced mom of three teenagers who e-mailed me. She was married for twelve years and chose to leave the relationship because her husband became an alcoholic and his disease threatened the well-being and safety of her family. In order to make ends meet, she has to work multiple jobs, seven days a week, doing things like housecleaning, pet sitting, nannying, and mystery shopping. She also sells items on eBay and Craigslist. Not only does she work hard doing these odd jobs, she also works hard to save and live as minimally as possible.

Here's the good news. Hard work does pay off. Let's hear this woman tell you in her own words.

Though it's been a rough three years, I'm happy to say that my hard work is paying off. I am almost 100 percent debt-free and that's even after paying for braces for my daughter. I am also saving for a down payment for my house (I'm halfway there!). As long as I continue to work hard as a single, self-employed mom, I'll make it. Juggling multiple jobs is hard, but I feel blessed to have all of them!

Sometimes we can't wait to create our ideal at-home business. We need the money now. Like this woman, if you are feeling the financial squeeze, do what it takes to bring home a paycheck and provide for your family. Even if it means temporarily juggling a few jobs. Even if it means doing something you don't particularly enjoy.

Focus on the progress you are making, even if it's just that you're not slipping further backward. Do what you *can* do and don't stress about what you *can't* do. Tiny steps in the right direction can add up to big change over time. Keep at it, keep counting your blessings, and keep moving forward.

3

The 8-to-5 Cure
Working for Yourself

A ship in harbor is safe, but that is
not what ships are built for.

—JOHN A. SHEDD, *SALT FROM MY ATTIC* (1928)

STEPHANIE IS A SINGLE WOMAN WHO WANTED TO START
her own business so she could support herself independently. She
researched and devoured books like *Good to Great* by Jim Collins
and *Rework* by Jason Fried. She then experimented with a number
of ideas including teaching piano, nannying, tutoring, baking bread,
desktop publishing, sewing pillowcases, cleaning houses, and playing
the harp at weddings.

While most of her ideas have been somewhat profitable, one of
them hit her a home run. An avid music lover, Stephanie discovered
that she really enjoyed playing the harp for weddings and special
events. Plus, she was paid well. To build her business, she began by

targeting the local market of brides, networking with wedding vendors, and attending bridal shows and other wedding conventions. Today, she is booked with high-paying gigs almost every single weekend.

The money Stephanie has earned from this business venture has allowed her to complete nursing school debt-free, and it has freed her to choose jobs in the medical field that she enjoys, rather than ones that simply pay the bills. She says, "When I file taxes, every year the income from my harp business is greater than the income from my work as a Certified Nurse Aid or as a Registered Nurse."

With multiple income streams and no student loans, Stephanie has flexibility in life. If she chooses, she can move anywhere and have little to no problem finding jobs in her field.

It makes me so happy to hear stories like this one. I just love how rewarding the entrepreneurial spirit can be and the far-reaching impact it can have on you and those around you. Whether you are single or married, there are many ways you can earn income, even if you don't want a regular full-time or part-time job.

While I don't believe that every woman needs to have a business or even make money in any capacity, I believe there are a number of reasons savvy home economists should consider looking for ways to increase their families' incomes. Maybe your family has debt you really want to pay off and your current income doesn't give you much wiggle room to attack your debt. Perhaps you are single or a single mom and are looking to establish more financial security. Or you might be looking for a way to increase your household income to give you some breathing room to be able to enjoy a few vacations or fun family outings each year. Maybe you are a mom whose kids are grown and gone and you are looking for a way to use your skills to make a difference or have more money to give generously.

There are many, many reasons for looking for ways to make more money, and there are many families and women who are searching out creative at-home options to give them more flexibility. Unfortunately, because many women do want to work from home, there are many scams out there (I'll talk about this in a bit). This is why it's important to make sure you are working for a reputable business or working for yourself.

What Is a Successful Business Idea?

If you're thinking of starting your own business, it is important to begin by defining what a successful business is. You need a target for which to aim before you even get started! Remember, a successful business is going to look different for different people. There is no one-size-fits-all path to getting there.

That said, I believe a successful business idea will hit the three following marks:

- provide steady income (This may take some time to develop— but this is the long-term goal!)
- be fulfilling, not exhausting
- play to your strengths

First, there is no point in starting a business or pursuing a business idea if it's not going to generate a profit. Your idea must consider the market for your product or service. Not only do you have to ask yourself if there are people out there who need whatever it is you have to offer, but you also have to consider if those same people are willing to pay for your product or service.

Keep in mind that financial success doesn't happen overnight. Don't expect to start making a load of money right off the bat. While it takes time, the long-term goal of any successful business should be to make a good and steady income for the hours you invest.

Second, your business idea must be satisfying. Don't bother investing the time and energy it will take if you don't enjoy what you do. All that fuels is frustration and stress. Also, if you envision working sixty to seventy hours a week all the time, sacrificing time spent with your family, feeling exhausted and burned out, and not having any downtime or margin for self-care, your idea is probably not worth pursuing.

Finally, your business idea must center on your strengths. I talked about that in the previous chapter. Doing something that does not align with what you are good at will likely end in failure.

In a minute I'll cover some groundwork that will provide the foundation for getting started. But first, let's discuss the realm of business opportunities.

What Are My Options?

In the previous chapter, I encouraged you to consider what your skills, talents, passions, and knowledge are. Defining those will give you a clearer picture of the business that might work for you. Let's look at some ways to run your own business.

Online Service or Product

An online business is run completely or primarily online. This a great option in this Internet-driven age. This includes online retailers or marketplaces (Etsy, eBay, Amazon); online services (graphic design, website design); virtual assistants (UpWork); technologists (creating iPhone and smartphone apps); and bloggers.

Melinda, one of my readers, has worked online in two different ventures for a number of years. For three years, she was an online tutor for a company called Brainfuse. She loved this opportunity because she was able to create her own schedule. In addition, for the past seven years, she has been purchasing infant and children's clothing at garage sales and thrift shops and reselling these items for a profit on eBay. Again, she's able to set her own hours and choose how much (or little) she works based upon the time and energy she has.

Pros:

- low start-up cost
- global target market
- flexible hours
- no commute

Cons:

- competitive market
- potentially long hours due to "being open" 24/7
- lonely (lack of social interaction and face-to-face connection)
- distractions (housework, children, unannounced visitors knocking on the door)

Home-Based, Face-to-Face Business

While any home-based business will likely involve the web on some level, there are certain jobs out there (or ones that you can create) that offer products or services that are not necessarily web-based except for having a website to advertise your services or products. Some face-to-face services include: dog sitting, working as a nanny, interior designing, or being a home organizer, life coach, consultant, or clothing designer.

For the past twenty or more years, Kristine has been cleaning houses. She works around sixteen hours total per week and is usually finished by the time her three kids get home from school. The income she's earned from this job has helped pay for vacations and allowed for margin in her family's budget.

Depending on the type of home-based, face-to-face business, the pros and cons of the business will vary.

Pros:

- flexible hours
- flexible "roaming retail" services (give clients and customers face time if they prefer)
- little to no commute

Cons:

- distractions (housework, children, unannounced visitors knocking on the door)
- figuring out how to set up an environment or space conducive to work
- may be costly, depending on services or products offered

Direct Sales Companies and Multi-Level Marketing

A sales business (think Thirty-One Gifts, Pampered Chef, dōTERRA, Young Living, and Mary Kay) can be run both offline and online, usually both. This type of business is especially great for those who love people, sales, and marketing.

Three years ago, Brittany started a business selling essential oils. She loves the opportunity to help people find more natural remedies for common health problems. Plus, she has done well income-wise! From the beginning, she's made around $500 per month with this business. While sales businesses require a lot of effort and cold calling, there is also great income potential.

Pros:

- high earning potential
- organization provides most start-up materials and training
- less financial risk if business fails

Cons:

- income generally based on how much you work
- high pressure to recruit; high-pressure sales strategies and methods
- higher rate of cynical customers

Brick-and-Mortar

A brick-and-mortar business is run out of a shop or physical space and is one that markets to your local community only. These include florists, bakeries, dry cleaners, restaurants, and music studios. Depending on what kind of products or services you offer, you may have no choice but to open your own store, especially if your products or services generate a high demand.

Gloria owns a clothing resale shop in the small town of Stockton, Illinois, called Glad Rags Boutique. She offers like-new, ready-to-wear clothing for the whole family. In addition, she has partnered with three tuxedo retailers to offer a full line of men's formal wear for rental or purchase. Before Gloria became the owner, she used to shop for her family's clothing at this consignment store. Twelve years ago, when she heard it was possibly going out of business, she purchased it in order to prevent it from being closed down.

She says:

> I am not always an outgoing person, but this store has given me the opportunity to meet someone new almost every day. Some people become regular customers, and of course, I have regular consignors as well. Some of these people would have never crossed my path other than me working daily at my store. Some of the relationships develop into a deeper friendship, and others are just in passing, but it is a joy to me to see how God uses those relationships in my life. I also love that because I am my own boss, I am always able to make the decision of closing the store, if needed, to be able to spend time with family or deal with family emergencies.

Pros:

- legitimacy due to physical location
- opportunity to supplement with online presence
- word-of-mouth advertisement can spread quickly in local community

Cons:

- limited customer base
- higher start-up cost (space, rent)
- long hours

Traditional

While this book targets non-traditional ways to generate income, it is worth noting that traditional work might be the path for you. Robyn e-mailed me with a great suggestion. She offers,

> For moms with kids who are in school, ask if you can work in the lunchroom. I started working at the beginning of the school year as a cafeteria/recess supervisor, which pays $19 an hour in our district. It's combat pay for sure, but only one hour a day! And, it led to me being offered another position in the district. I'll be working in an elementary school library in the same school district as my kids, with the same hours as my youngest. Same days off, same holidays, and full benefits (which we desperately need)!

If you'd prefer to take a more traditional route before venturing out on your own, consider looking for part-time work in your local or nearby community, whether for a corporate company, local government, or a retail store.

Take 5

By now, you may have a rough idea of what you can do or you may be tossing around different ideas that might work. Before you move forward and begin to explore your options, I encourage you to ask yourself the following five questions:

1. Am I so passionate about this idea that I'm willing to put in the work to see it through?

Your idea needs to be your brainchild, something you are

wholeheartedly excited about and in love with. Because, believe me, you're going to need that passion on those long and hard days when you feel like giving up.

I will never forget an e-mail I received a few years back from a woman I didn't know. She told me she wanted to start a website that was similar to mine, but she was having trouble coming up with a name. She said she didn't have any ideas at all, but figured I probably had some. Her request: could I please tell her some of my best name ideas so she could use one of them for her website?

While I love helping budding entrepreneurs and try to answer as many questions e-mailed to me as I can, I didn't take the time to respond to this woman's e-mail. Why? Well, had this woman e-mailed with a list of possible names and a succinct vision for her site, I would have been happy to offer some input. However, she didn't appear as if she wanted to work hard or was invested enough to put in time, thought, and effort to see her idea succeed; it seemed she just wanted me to give her my best ideas so she could use one of them.

If you're hoping someone else will give you a big leg up with getting a business started, I can almost guarantee you that you're not going to be successful. That might sound harsh, but I stand behind this statement. Successful business owners take initiative. They put in backbreaking effort and hard work. They don't wait for others to spoon-feed their success. They make things happen.

2. Who is my potential customer?

Once you land on an idea that has a potential market, the next step is to define that market. Don't just say, "My business is going to help everyone." That is rarely true. Instead, your business is going to meet the needs of a specific type of person. Do yourself a favor from the start and define who that person is.

For instance, before I write a book or release a product, one of the exercises I do is create a fictitious person to represent the potential customer or reader. I decide how old she is, what her personality is, how many children she likely has, and more. This might seem a little over-the-top, but it really helps me solidify for whom my book or product is created. When I can picture a face for my target market, then I am able to write the book or create the product to meet the specific needs of that person.

You cannot meet the needs of everyone with every product, so define your market from the beginning. This will help you determine the best approach to target your intended audience. Reaching teen guys versus middle-aged moms, for example, takes a completely different strategy.

3. Can I afford the start-up costs?

While many may disagree, I strongly believe that you should never go into debt to start a business. If you do, you're launching with a noose around your neck. And that's not a good place to begin.

If you don't have the money needed for the start-up costs, go back to the drawing board and downsize your idea, or save aggressively for six months or more in order to have the cash necessary to cover all of the start-up costs. Ideally, you'll want to be able to cover the first three to six months' worth of costs with your savings, without even making a dime of profit.

Not only will this cushion relieve a lot of stress that is often involved with starting a business, it will also allow you to invest some or all of your initial profits back into the business. This will give you an even stronger foundation for your business.

Looking for some ideas to build up some cash, whether to invest in a website, material for your product, or a place to set up shop? Here are a few things for you to consider:

- Go through your house and sell items you no longer need. Hold a yard sale. De-clutter and make money at the same time.
- Significantly cut your budget for a season. Think extreme. And think temporary. Stop eating out. Don't buy new clothes. Challenge yourself to save every dollar you can.
- Temporarily work an extra or part-time job. Use the money you make to put into your new idea.
- If you have to buy supplies or products, do it as lean as possible. Buy used. Make do with what you have until you can afford to purchase something better or more.

4. Have I done enough research?

Most people are so eager to jump ahead and start a business that they don't take enough time to do the necessary research. I recommend that you read at least ten to twenty business-related books before you move forward with your idea. (I'll include some of my favorite books in the Resources section at the end of this book.) The knowledge you learn will help you shape your business and create a solid action plan.

Also, talk to everyone you know who has started a business or who works in the field or industry you'd like to enter. Tell them about your business idea, ask them for input, and pick their brains on the lessons they've learned along the way. This counsel could prove invaluable. Truly, every great idea I've ever come up with has been initially sparked by something I read or someone I talked to.

Don't be afraid to ask questions. Reading Ken Coleman's book, *One Question*, inspired me to ask well-crafted questions. One quote that I loved from the book was, "Good questions inform. Great questions transform." Getting the right answer often starts with asking the right question, not a broad or vague one. Think about what you need to learn or want to know and ask specific questions around those topics.

For instance, ask,

"What do you enjoy most about owning your own business?"

"What are some of your biggest challenges?"

"How do you acquire new clients?"

Then, genuinely listen to the answers and ask follow-up questions. You'll learn so much!

One last thing: keep an open mind. Don't assume that because some people are in completely different industries or markets that they don't have valuable information to share. In fact, some of those very people will have some of the best ideas. My husband, Jesse, suggested that I start a Facebook page way back when few bloggers had them. I wasn't entirely convinced—especially because he doesn't know a lot about blogging—but I figured it wouldn't hurt to try. Well, Jesse's suggestion turned out to be brilliant! In fact, Facebook is consistently one of our top sources of blog traffic every month with, at the time of this writing, over 750,000 followers. His seemingly crazy idea turned out to be a crazy-good idea!

5. *Am I willing to fail?*

If you take the leap of faith and try new things, you are going to fail at least some of the time. Expect to succeed, but willingly accept failure. Not every business idea is going to be a slam dunk success. In fact, most of them won't be.

As I talked about in the previous chapter, when I was pregnant with my first child and had to stop working, we took a huge hit in our income. As I was trying to get my wedding business off the ground, I considered other part-time things I could do from home. One idea I had was to teach creative writing classes out of our home. I had always loved writing and figured that local homeschool moms would jump at the opportunity to enroll their children in creative writing classes—especially if they were inexpensively priced.

I was stoked and expected big things! I spent hours writing up advertisements to place in homeschool newsletters. I had visions of at least forty children signing up. I excitedly strategized how I could break the classes up. I eagerly calculated numbers, anticipating a good earning potential from these classes.

Problem was, not everyone in the community shared my enthusiasm.

Instead of forty children signing up as I had hoped, only four signed on. So much for my big plans! I worried about how on earth we were going to pay our bills since my fabulous idea had pretty much bombed. I wanted to throw my hands up and quit. But I couldn't. I had made a commitment to teach these children—all four of them—and I had to see it through.

When I look back at those classes and the measly four sign-ups, I realize that not only did that experience prepare me for some greater failures I would have down the road, it also taught me that it's okay if things don't turn out as expected. I could still carry on and do my best whether I taught four students, forty students, or four hundred students. Whatever the outcome of our efforts, what matters most is that we give it our best.

Sometimes our brilliant ideas don't automatically come to fruition. Alexa learned this very thing. Here is what she has to say about what finally worked for her:

In the summer of 2012 I got divorced and my two kids and I moved in with my dad. I was working two jobs at the time and was on the verge of a mental breakdown.

I tried a number of online businesses before one finally stuck: writing blog posts for companies. When I first decided to give this a try I was working as a personal lines insurance agent. Since I knew a lot about insurance, I decided to target insurance agencies and insurance marketing companies.

I would simply do a Google search for insurance agencies with a blog and then if I found an agency that didn't have regular blog updates I would e-mail them letting them know I could help. I'd also respond to job ads on job boards (mainly the ProBlogger.net job board) for anything insurance related. I got most of the insurance types of jobs because I was an agent.

After building up my portfolio I started expanding into personal finance. If I saw a personal finance website with many authors I'd simply e-mail the owner to see if they needed another writer.

By October of 2013, I finally had enough writing clients to completely quit my day jobs and freelance full-time. I had been making around $2,500 per month for the past year or so and this month I'll finally have cracked the $3,000 mark.

To make a long story short, I now make more than what I was earning from both of my day jobs combined. I purchased a trailer for my daughters and me to live in and put it on an extra lot my dad had. I don't make a lot of money from my online business (yet) but I feel like I've provided for my daughters and I have allowed myself to have a schedule where I can be there for them. Which to me is the best thing in the world.

I've slowly learned over the past few years that when you have your own business or are trying to start working from home, failure of some kind is inevitable. This may be sobering to some of you, and while I'm not intentionally trying to dampen your optimism and visions of grandeur, the truth is, building something from scratch is usually a lot harder and a lot less successful than we plan or hope for.

However, contrary to what I thought in the beginning, I've come to realize that failure is my friend. I've learned much more through failure than I have through success. As a matter of fact, without my experience in failing, I would have never had the opportunity to start my blog, MoneySavingMom.com.

Remember, success is almost always guaranteed to those who are willing to try, try again. Even if your first or third or fifth idea doesn't work, you'll eventually land on something that will be a success.

Dos and Don'ts of a Successful Business

As you begin planning to launch your business, here are some rules and guidelines to consider:

Do Your Homework

Don't take your business venture lightly. Rushing into anything without careful planning and research is a way to set yourself up for failure. Take time to research business laws that apply to your idea. You will probably need to consider one or more of the following to legitimize your venture:

- specific licenses or permits for your business or product offerings
- zoning laws for a physical office location
- legal registration of your business under the appropriate entity (that is, S corp or LLC)
- procurement of a federal tax ID number and setup of a separate bank account used solely for business income and expenses
- Check out the U.S. Small Business Administration (SBA .gov) for great starter advice and guidance as well as state-specific requirements and information. They offer "how to start a _____ business" kits that cover a wide variety of business types and ideas. They also offer free consulting to help you get started. My friend Joy and her sister, Jen, own The Cupcake Tower—a business that offers custom cupcake stands. Joy told me that when she and her sister were first starting their business, they contacted SBA.gov and were able to get free consulting advice from retired CEOs who volunteer with the SBA.

In addition, I recommend contacting your local Small Business Administration office to let them know the kind of business you are planning to start and to ask if there are any licenses you need to obtain or anything you need to know to start your proposed business. Depending on the size and nature of your business, it may also be wise to talk to an attorney who has experience helping small business owners so you can get input on how to legally structure your business. Most attorneys will offer a free consultation via phone or in person to briefly discuss your needs and options.

I also strongly encourage you to meet with an accountant to get guidance on federal and state-specific tax issues, bookkeeping, and anything else you need to consider for your unique business idea and situation.

Do Set a Few Scary Goals

It's good to take risks. It's good to do hard things. It's good to push ourselves. And it's good to step outside our comfort zones. So when you're starting out, set goals that scare you, at least a little.

If you always stay where it's easy and safe, you'll miss a lot of interesting and exciting opportunities. You'll never reach your full potential. And you'll also become stagnant. You'll grow old sitting at the starting gate waiting for the gun to go off.

When I began writing this book, I set a scary goal to get a solid draft of the manuscript written in less than three months. If you know anything about writing a book, it's not an easy task and this was a really, really tight deadline. But I set that audacious goal knowing it would push and motivate me to get it done more quickly. Even if I didn't hit that deadline, I knew I'd have a much greater head start on the book than had I not set the scary goal.

Corinne and her husband set a scary goal to pay off their student loans in one year. They have made much progress so far and are actually ahead of schedule. She writes,

> We've sold things, done bake sales, and earned extra here and there. I'm amazed at how much we've been able to pay off of our student loan already! All by setting a goal that seemed unrealistic.

If setting scary goals seems, well, scary right now, begin by setting a few small goals to help propel your idea into reality. After all, if you don't know where you want to go, how will you know when you've gotten there? If you don't live with purposeful intention, aimlessness will be the default.

One thing that has been amazingly effective for me is to set specific goals for our businesses: from the income we hope to generate in a week, month, or year to detailed projects we hope to accomplish in a specific time frame. We don't just set big goals; we also break these down into bite-sized chunks.

One of my first online money-making ventures was to resell books I had purchased wholesale. I sold these on my own website, as well as on eBay. Because it was a new business and I didn't have a big customer base built, I set a goal to make $200 each week. This meant that I had to make forty dollars each weekday. Once I had this goal on paper, I started to brainstorm every free option I could contrive to drive more traffic and sales to my site. Some of them worked, some of them didn't, but had I not had that very specific goal, I doubt I would have been as driven to be creative.

Our business goals propel us to constantly tweak our processes so that we are more efficient in running our businesses. They motivate us to look for out-of-the-box marketing ideas. And they challenge us to not be content with the status quo.

Where do you hope to be financially in a year from now? How about three years from now? What about five years from now?

Choose two or three specific financial goals for the next few years and start thinking of practical ways you can get there. What can you do outside of your 8-to-5 job to build additional income streams? When can you start? What do you need to do to make your idea work? How big of a customer base do you need? How much do you have to save for your start-up costs and by when? When do you need your website up and running? What kind of marketing will you do?

Once you have your big goals written down on paper, break them down into bite-sized monthly and weekly chunks. Don't be afraid to be specific. Even if you don't come close to hitting them, you'll be much farther along than if you didn't try at all.

Do Be Willing to Sacrifice

Starting a business is going to require sacrifices, especially in the beginning season. There are going to be time sacrifices and monetary sacrifices. You need to consider how much money and time you have to invest.

And sometimes sacrifice means more than that. It can mean stretching yourself outside of your comfort zone or education or job qualifications in order to discover other options.

I recently received an e-mail from a stay-at-home mom. A graphic/web designer by trade, she was interested in part-time work but wasn't able to gain much traction finding work in that particular field. Her goal was to replenish her savings account and start digging her family out of debt to be able to save for a house. She felt hopeless trying to find a job that fit her exact qualifications.

In her case, I believe she needed to generate an idea on her own, something that wasn't dependent on finding availability in a certain job or company. Yes, that means this woman would need to stretch herself mentally and sacrifice her comfort zone to research other options. Remember, finding clever ways to make money is not going to be easy at first. But the payoff (sometimes the literal one) is worth it.

Do Experiment, Experiment, Experiment!

There are many different job opportunities available, so don't be afraid to try something new. And then if that doesn't work, try something else.

For most of her working life, Gayle has had a part-time side job in addition to her full-time job. She says:

> I have helped a small local business owner reconcile the books each month; I have conducted telephone surveys for a research company; I have delivered Sunday newspapers before the crack of dawn; I have been hired by a neighbor to sort through their garage full of stuff and run a garage sale (keeping 50 percent of the profits); and I've helped my wedding organizer friend haul flowers and decorations on Saturdays during the spring and summer—her busy seasons. There are many options out there!

I love how willing Gayle is to experiment with a bunch of different possibilities. It works for her and can work for you!

Do Say Yes

Sometimes opportunities—*good* opportunities—will come your way that you haven't even been looking for. Some people might approach you for help because they recognize your value, skills, homemade product, or expertise. Don't immediately say no. Take time to investigate the opportunity. Ask questions. See where it leads. Following is an inspiring e-mail that I received from Linnea, a woman grateful for having said yes.

I felt compelled to write to you about my home business that I started about 14 years ago. My business name is Sewing Services: Police-Sheriff-Fire. I began this business when our daughter was about 4 years old.

The local police department approached me about doing sewing and alterations for them. I have had a passion for sewing ever since I was in 4-H where I learned the basics of garment construction. Not really believing that this request would amount to much, but knowing that this would be a way to pay for the "extras" that we might want in our lives, I decided to give this offer a try. Admittedly, at that point, I wasn't sure I wanted to work with law enforcement. I thought of police as being rather "cold" and distant.

To my absolute amazement, my workload was far more than I expected; other law enforcement and fire agencies began to call me for services. And I fell in love with our public servants who keep our communities safe. What can I say? They stole my heart. Never in the last 14 years have I had to advertise. I even have a back-up seamstress who helps me when I get overwhelmed.

· What I love most about this woman saying yes, despite her initial hesitation, was what she told me toward the end of her e-mail. Linnea wrote how her work created in her a desire to contribute to her local community. She began volunteering with the police department's Crisis Intervention Team, a program that offers training for police officers to work with people who have a mental illness or mental impairment and who are in crisis.

Do Something

In Seth Godin's book *Poke the Box*, he challenges people to stop spending so much time researching, planning, and goal setting. Instead, he suggests you just go out and do something. Stop staying stuck in a box; bust through walls and make things happen.

I'm undoubtedly a big advocate of doing a lot of research ahead of just jumping into any business idea, but I also believe wholeheartedly that you learn much more through hands-on experimentation than you can ever learn through reading about something or taking a class about it. So do your homework, get good counsel from others who have run businesses before, and read as many business books as you can get your hands on, but don't spend so much time planning, brainstorming, and preparing to launch that you never actually push the start button.

Don't Fall for Scams

Mei, one of my blog followers, wrote to me about wanting to earn money, but based on her previous experience she worried about advertising scams. She writes,

In the past I've bought into the scams of stuffing envelopes or assembling crafts at home for extra income. Both of these so-called opportunities were definite scams and I didn't make a penny. However, I didn't let that stop me from trying again. Since I have been a crafter since I was very young, when I saw an ad for making extra money at home assembling crafts, I figured that would be an easy one for me to do and something that I already enjoyed doing.

Mei paid for the mail-order assembly kit and eagerly waited for it to arrive. When she got it in the mail, the assembly consisted of a particular number of cheap straw hats, ribbons, and flowers. The instructions were simple: glue a ribbon around a hat and then glue a flower on the ribbon. Seems idiotproof, right? Especially for someone who is naturally crafty. Well, after Mei submitted her finished kits to the company, she received a letter back from a "supervisor" saying she would not receive any compensation because the flowers were placed incorrectly. Since Mei had followed the directions perfectly, she knew this couldn't be right. It was then that she realized she had fallen for a scam.

Mei is not alone in suffering the disappointment that comes when you realize you invested time and money in something that wasn't authentic. Ever notice how many messages about how you can make hundreds of dollars a week working from home clutter your inbox or junk mail folder? Yes, scams are out there. In fact, they are everywhere. Some are easy to dismiss, but others can look legitimate and convince you that, yes, you can make a lot of money, starting now, doing practically nothing. These offers are akin to e-mails advertising weight loss products that claim you can eat anything, all day, and still lose weight.

The best way to determine a scam is by researching the business.

Ask around. Check out the company on the Better Business Bureau's website (BBB.org). Do a Google search for the business name and the word *scam*. Finally, if the opportunity demands that you invest a significant amount of money up front, beware.

Don't Feel Discouraged

A mom of a baby and a toddler recently e-mailed me in desperation, with many tears and much frustration as she communicated her struggle trying to attain financial freedom. She said:

> I want so badly to find a way to earn money from home, but it feels like I just can't ever quite find a way to do it. Just when I think that I've discovered an idea that will work, something comes along and sets me back. I think my biggest struggle is not the limited hours I have to work because of my children, but the deep-seated fear and insecurity I've had since my childhood.

In the past, she tried a number of different business ideas, including working for a multi-level marketing company, working the overnight shift, and delivering newspapers in the early morning. These admirable attempts at bringing in income either never took off or left her so exhausted she could barely drag herself out of bed to take care of her kids.

I want to give women like this one some grace to help relieve the pressure.

Let's face it. Life isn't perfect. Our schedules aren't perfect. Our living situations aren't perfect. Our timetables aren't perfect. Some of you may have no trouble launching your business idea. Others of you may find it more challenging (though still doable!). Don't stress if you're in the latter bunch.

Some of us are in seasons of our lives where our responsibilities seem maxed out. We are caring for newborns, helping with aging parents, tending to family members who are sick, and time wise we can't afford to put in even a ten-or twenty-hour workweek.

Do the best with what you can. As I've said before, do something. Start small. And when your life season affords more breathing space, pick up the pace. Do what you can, when you can, where you are!

Don't Give Up

Babe Ruth said, "It's hard to beat a person who never gives up."[1] When I started Covenant Wedding Source, my long-term goal was to build a business that would earn a part-time side income and allow me to stay home while my husband was in law school. I never would have dreamed that ten years later, I would be running a large blog, writing books, speaking to audiences around the country, and have an amazing team working for me.

Many times, people look at me and only see the accomplishments and successes. What they don't see are the hours, days, weeks, months, and years I worked very (very) hard and saw little return on my investment. They don't see the many (many) times I've come inches away from shutting it all down from frustration and discouragement.

The success of MoneySavingMom.com is not because I'm really smart (if you only knew how much I struggled with math in school!) or because I'm naturally techie (I would be nowhere without my tech team!) or because I have a master's degree in marketing (I didn't even go to college!).

I believe wholeheartedly that plain ole hard work and perseverance have been the key ingredients for the success of my business. I just plain refuse to give up. This doesn't mean that I don't sometimes scrap ideas that flop (I do—often!), but this means that even when it's hard, even when I experience setback and failure, I am committed to keep plugging away, to keep experimenting, and to keep learning and growing.

Early on in my blogging journey, I had an experience that tested my fortitude and commitment to being in business for myself. A year after we started MoneySavingMom.com, a large international retail company hired a group of twelve frugal bloggers and paid them to record videos on saving money and to upload those videos to their site. Because I had been working with this company on some projects at the time and was also closely connected with a few of the bloggers, I found out about this project early on. It sounded like a great idea (I'm all about encouraging people to save money!). The problem was that the domain name this company had chosen to host these videos was MoneySavingMoms.com—exactly the same as my domain name, only with an added *s* at the end. I should have known better from the beginning and purchased that name myself, but I didn't think to do so. Live and learn, right?

As if to add insult to injury, not only were these bloggers asked to actively promote this new site on their own blogs, but this retail giant advertised this group on the bottom of every single one of their store receipts nationwide. Then, they launched a nationwide Money Saving Moms Contest.

I was unsure what to do. On the one hand, I knew that in a court of law I could prove first use of the name "Money Saving Mom" since my site had been set up and actively run for a year. Legally, even though I didn't have a federal trademark, because I had been using the name in commerce for longer than this company had, I owned the common law trademark.

On the other hand, it was overwhelming to think of pitting myself against an international brand that was massively bigger than me with more legal and financial resources than I could even dream of. I was a tiny gnat in their universe, and frankly, I felt as though I couldn't tell them to stop using the name. Jesse and I knew whatever small amount of money we had saved would get drained pretty quickly if we pursued legal action.

But the hard truth was, if we didn't do something, it was slowly going to kill my brand! Internet searches for "Money Saving Mom" and certain other related terms resulted in their website popping up before my site on search pages. I knew that the more time passed and the bigger they built their site, the less of a chance I would have to continue building my brand and site. I could see the writing on the wall—and it spelled impending business disaster.

In the middle of wondering what on earth I was going to do about this unexpected situation, one of the employees from this company e-mailed me and said in so many words, "We hope you are okay with our new site and the fact that the name is almost the same as yours." Um, no. I wasn't okay. But I did feel pretty powerless.

Long story short, after exchanging a few e-mails with the retail giant and getting nowhere, we talked to an attorney who assured us we were in the legal right because we owned the common law trademark and could prove it. After a lot of deliberation and prayer, we got courageous and sent an e-mail that politely asked this company to remove the name from their site, shut down MoneySavingMoms .com, remove the link to the site on their store receipts, and discontinue using it, or we would be forced to take legal action.

To this day, it sounds crazy that little ole me sent such a gutsy e-mail, but I just couldn't stand by and watch my hard work dissipate without putting up a fight. Much to our shock, they backed down. Apparently, their legal team knew they didn't have a case, they were just waiting for us to call them out on it. Almost immediately, they scrubbed their website of all references to "Money Saving Moms" and profusely—shocking!—apologized that it would take them nine days to remove the reference off their store receipts.

We were ecstatic, amazed, and blown away! Had we tucked our tails between our legs and surrendered without a fight, it's likely our business would not exist today. But we didn't give up. And we didn't lose heart or faith, even though we were face-to-face with a gigantic worldwide retailer. This victory fueled my courage and continually reminds me to not run away or give up when that seems like the much easier option.

Maybe over the years you've had a flurry of fits and starts but nothing worked out. Maybe the last business idea you had cost you more money and time than you could afford. Maybe the idea of launching your company seems like something that will take forever.

Whatever your situation, I want to encourage you to not give up. You may need to change your plans, tweak your dreams, or alter your course. You might need to shelve the idea and start a new one. You may need to extend the deadline or revise the game plan. That's all part of learning and growing.

But no matter what, don't give up. Winners aren't quitters. Keep going, keep pressing forward, keep learning, keep experimenting, and someday soon, you will start to see fruit from your effort.

4

Get Moving, Start Building

Even if you are on the right track, you'll
get run over if you just sit there.

—WILL ROGERS

EVER SINCE SHE COULD REMEMBER, LIZANNE FALSETTO
had wanted to be a fashion model. When she turned seventeen, she
signed with an agency in Japan and left her Seattle hometown for far-
away Tokyo. For the next ten years, she pursued her dream, modeling
across the span of the globe.

Due to her fast-paced, on-the-go lifestyle, Lizanne was always on
the lookout for a healthy snack she could pack in her purse, but there
was nothing on the market that was as nutritious as she wanted.
Lizanne decided to stop searching and make her own. She was no
stranger to the kitchen, hailing from a large, traditional Italian
family who shared a deep love and passion for cooking and eating.
Engrained in her memory are the hearty dinners they indulged in
together that usually lasted for hours.

Lizanne began experimenting with her grandmother's most-requested cookie recipe, eliminating unhealthy ingredients and replacing them with good stuff. Soon enough, she created her own protein bar that was rich in protein and other nutrients, had no sugar, and was gluten free. Friends and fellow models who tried the snack loved it and always asked for more.

At the end of her modeling career, Lizanne moved back to the States. Settling in Los Angeles, she wondered what she was going to do with the rest of her life. Together with a food consultant, she decided to tweak her recipe and create a nutrition bar called think-Thin. There is so much more to this story, but I am amazed at how a simple idea that started in the kitchen ultimately turned into a booming company that in 2012 reached just over $70 million in sales and is continuing to grow.[1]

In chapter 2, we talked about the importance of coupling what you're good at with an existing need in a market that you can fill. And in the previous chapter, you learned about the possibilities and options of starting your own business as a way to increase your household income.

While there are multiple ways to make money other than running your own business, if this is the route you intend to take, this chapter will offer practical tips to help you get out of the gate and well on your way to success. If you are not yet totally sold or interested in starting your own business as a way of supplementing your finances, you will still glean insight (and in the next chapter I will continue to offer a slew of other non-traditional ideas and tips).

It's important to note that because there are countless business ideas out there, it is impossible to offer you a step-by-step plan tailored to your particular idea. I encourage you to find specific resources (books, podcasts, blogs, websites) that align with what you decide to do. I'll share a list of some of my favorites at the end of this book.

Determine Your Why (a.k.a. Your Mission Statement)

You've probably heard the term "mission statement" many times in the course of your life. It may seem like something that's boring, hokey, or inconsequential. But here's the thing: if you can't explain to me in two sentences or less what your business is about, you won't be able to develop a clear action plan and specific strategies to implement your plan.

Not too long ago, I was at a writer's conference that offered would-be authors the opportunity to connect with agents and publishers in order to hopefully procure a mutually beneficial book deal. Many publishers attended the event and scheduled meetings with budding writers.

The problem? Very few of the writers had a concise and unique "pitch" for their book. I know because I interacted with many of these men and women at lunch, after sessions, and during breaks. When I asked them, "What is your book about?" the majority of them responded with vague, long-winded, beat-around-the-bush answers. Granted, these same folks had amazing stories, great passion, and a burning desire to write a book. But few had a polished and clear-cut purpose for what kind of book they wanted to write (or were writing) and why. I loved their hearts, but I was sad to think that their lack of defining and refining their proposed book idea was probably going to hurt their chances of getting a book deal.

Enthusiasm, excitement, and determination won't get you anywhere if you don't know where you are going.

When I first started working on this book manuscript, my number one priority was to define what the book was going to be about. I didn't want to hem and haw anytime anyone asked about the subject matter. Nor did I want a theoretical and illusive definition. I wanted it to be clear and direct. (By the way, some people call this an elevator pitch, when you can articulately summarize an idea in about thirty seconds, the time it would take you to ride up or down an elevator with someone.)

It took time and discussion with my team members, friends, and husband, in addition to a lot of personal reflection and consideration, to finally land on my pitch for this book. I was thrilled to be able to effectively communicate the one-sentence objective for this book when asked, which was "to encourage women with practical ways they could increase their income, multiply their impact, and not lose their joy in the process."

Crafting this mission statement allowed me to begin writing with confidence and precision. I knew exactly what my end goal was for this book and could focus my energy on making that happen.

Before you begin to think about what your next steps are, what you need to get in place to launch, and how you're going to market your idea, I urge you to take a step back and craft a concise statement to represent your business.

To help draft your mission statement, consider the needs you are going to meet or the problems you are going to solve through your business. I talked about this in chapter one.

Successful businesses aren't just ideas that sound great; they fill a void or solve problems that people deal with on a regular basis. If your proposed business idea isn't doing any one of these things, there's a good chance it's not going to succeed.

When people ask me what MoneySavingMom.com is all about,

I always reply, "We serve as a one-stop shop to help busy women save money and live their lives with intention." Can you pinpoint the needs we serve through this statement? They include things such as:

- money worries
- budgeting
- finding fulfillment
- living with purpose
- the challenges of time-crunched living

Everything we do at MoneySavingMom.com aims to fulfill our mission statement. By defining it, we know what we're about. And we also know what we're *not* about.

Almost every day, we have opportunities pitched to us, either for guest posts people want to write, companies who want to work with us, event coordinators who want me to speak at their upcoming events, or media outlets that want to interview me. By knowing what we're about, we are able to accept only the opportunities that are in line with our mission statement. This is part of what makes us an intentional business.

A mission statement helps you to refine and define what your business is about. It allows you to stay focused on your target. As you think about your mission statement, let's read a few from some well-known companies. You'll see how each example encompasses what the business is about and is clear about the needs it fills.

IKEA

At IKEA our vision is to create a better everyday life for the many people. Our business idea supports this vision by offering a wide range of well-designed, functional home furnishing products at prices so low that as many people as possible will be able to afford them.[2]

Trader Joe's

The mission of Trader Joe's is to give our customers the best food and beverage values that they can find anywhere and to provide them with the information required to make informed buying decisions. We provide these with a dedication to the highest quality of customer satisfaction delivered with a sense of warmth, friendliness, fun, individual pride, and company spirit. Quoted in Lindsay Kolowich, "9 Truly Inspiring Company Mission Statement Examples," Hubspot, August 20, 2014, accessed July 21, 2015, http://blog.hubspot.com/marketing/inspiring-company-mission-statements.

Harris Teeter

The Harris Teeter aim is to be absolutely the best grocery retailer as measured by each and every customer. The Harris Teeter mission is to: take excellent care [of] our customers; take excellent care of our fellow associates; keep our stores clean; sell only fresh products; keep our shelves properly stocked.[3]

Define Your How (a.k.a. Your Action Plan)

After you've decided upon your mission statement, you're ready to draft your action plan. If you read any business books or attend classes on how to start a business, one of the first things you'll hear is the concept of creating a business plan. This is a detailed layout of how you intend to fund your business, how quickly you anticipate it will grow, and how much income you estimate you'll make. While I think there is value in creating a business plan to think about your long-term dreams for the business, I believe a business *action* plan is much more valuable.

In the previous chapter, I stressed the importance of doing your research. Have you talked to other people in your particular field who can offer specialized advice? Have you bounced your idea around to others? Have you researched the market to determine what value you can offer and where you fit in? Have you determined the particular licenses or qualifications you will need to run your business? The research you have done will help you answer the following questions that will frame your action plan:

1. What kind of business will you run? Online? At-home? Brick-and-mortar? Direct sales?
2. How are you going to fulfill your mission statement?
3. What is going to make your business stand out from your competitors?

It's not enough to dream; you need to *do*. Turn your dreams into realistic execution steps. In increments of three months, six months, and one year, think about and answer the following questions:

1. What do you want your business to accomplish?
2. How big do you want it to be?
3. How much income do you want it to produce?
4. How much product do you want to sell?
5. How many hours do you want to work per week?

Because this is preliminary planning, some of these answers may simply be guesses; but this is your first step to determine your action plan and the goals it will require.

After you've answered the above questions, downsize these big goals into smaller, executable chunks. Think about what you need to do now in order to reach those mile markers.

For instance, let's say you want to start a cake decorating business. You'll want to start by setting the date you'll open your doors to the public. If it's six months from now, work backward to determine your action steps. You will probably need to do the following:

- research food handling laws
- find a commercial kitchen or space to use
- take some classes
- create a website
- design advertising materials (fliers, business cards, local ads)
- network with other local businesses (party planning companies, catering halls, and so on)

If you want to open a day care in your home, you will probably need to do the following:

- research and procure appropriate state licensing and other requirements.
- create a play-oriented, child-proof space
- design policies and procedures for children and parents
- advertise and market your day care
- purchase toys, books, and furnishings

- plan out how your daily routine will look
- seek advice from other people who run day cares

Regardless of the business you are pursuing, you probably have a list of items running rampant in your head or notes that you've jotted down of things that need to be done to get your business on its feet. They may include the following items:

- create a website
- advertise and market your services and products
- buy supplies
- target potenital customers
- create a blog
- build a social media platform

Some of you have long lists of different goals and actions to execute, but you feel stuck. You may be overwhelmed and lack clarity on where to start. If I'm describing you, ask yourself, "What is the most important thing right now?" For instance, building a website may initially be more important than creating your product. Or, creating your product may be more important than acquiring customers. Then, ask yourself, "What is next?"

These two questions will help you create and follow a road map to bring your idea to fruition. Once you answer the first question, follow with the next one, then repeat. This process will also help you keep the momentum going.

I'm frequently asked, "Crystal, how do you do it all?" I think the important thing to remember is that I have slowly added new things—like Facebook, Twitter, an e-mail newsletter, and so on—to my plate. If I had tried to set up everything all at once, I would have been completely overwhelmed, and probably not have done a very good job.

Don't try to do everything at once. The best way to avoid getting burned out or stuck is to start with one thing at a time. You can't dive headfirst into social media, network with your local community to drum up business, and learn how to maximize traffic on your website all at the same time (and do it well). Stick with one action item, and when you are comfortable with your pace and progress, continue to the next step.

When I created my Facebook page for MoneySavingMom.com, it took a lot of time and thought to regularly update it at first. I had to learn how to post links and different types of posts, what worked best, and what types of posts were most effective. Then, I had to practice doing it over and over again. As I continue to update my Facebook page on a daily basis, it has become something I do without much thought. It's almost as habitual as brushing my teeth. Now, I'm just as excited and dedicated to doing it, but it doesn't take anywhere near as long as it used to.

Pace yourself when you start setting up your business. Challenge yourself to try new things little by little. Don't implement every action item for your business at once. Pick one or two things to focus on at a time before you start experimenting with new ideas or implementing new goals.

Things to Think About

As you take the beginning steps to set up your business, here are some building blocks to consider including in your action plan.

Brand Development

Don't rush through this part of the process. In fact, I'd say this is the most important thing to consider once you know what your business is going to be about.

Branding is crucial. Think about it this way—you don't just represent your brand; you *are* your brand.

The name you choose for your business and website should (1) encompass your mission and (2) clearly articulate the purpose of your business. I have found it helpful to make a list of all the possibilities. Brainstorm and write down every name and idea that comes to mind. It doesn't matter if an idea seems silly or crazy, just write it down. Get your creative juices flowing.

As I mentioned before, don't rush into a decision. Take a week or two to consider potential names. Ask a few trusted friends to give their input. Think long-term. Is your name going to allow your business to grow? Do you absolutely love it? Say it over and over again. Picture it on big screens, billboards, websites, and magazine covers. Do you still love it? Is there anything about it that just doesn't seem right? If so, go back to the drawing board and keep trying. Eventually, the name will come.

Word to the wise: don't use weird spellings. They might be cute, but they aren't practical when people are trying to look up your business online. For instance, about a year before I started MoneySavingMom .com, I started a frugal-living site called SimplyCentsible.com. It was a fun play on words but a nightmare for people to search for and remember (and while I don't necessarily think it was entirely the name's fault, the site never got off the ground). If you have to spell your business name out letter by letter when you tell people about it, you should probably consider another name.

In the same vein, it's becoming more popular to use a name that is a made-up word (think Google, eBay, or Pinterest). While these can work well if your brand takes off, in most cases, I think it's much better to choose a name that actually tells others what the business is about. If your name defines you, you are well on your way to establishing a strong brand.

Many will disagree with me, but I believe that unless you are a celebrity, someone with a large offline following, or have written bestselling books, it's usually better to choose a name that encompasses your business mission instead of using your actual name. People won't think to search for your name if they don't know it, but they will think to search for the topics you are writing about.

Brand strategy and design firm Lippincott created the name Sprite for the citrusy Coca-Cola soft drink. Stemming from the Latin word *spiritus*, for spirit, it means "elf, fairy, or goblin." When the product was released in 1961, it was marketed as something refreshing, lively, and energetic. What a perfect name! The same company also came up with Verizon. It combined the Latin word for truth, *veritas*, with *horizon*. The combo created a name that suggested a reliable and forward-thinking company.

Ever hear of the company Stat.us? Of course you haven't! But back when Twitter was still an idea, this was the original name the folks in the boardroom came up with. Cofounder Jack Dorsey wasn't pleased with the branding results and eventually settled on Twitter, defined in the dictionary as "a short burst of inconsequential information." Fitting, wouldn't you say?

Back in 2007 when we were first brainstorming ideas for a frugal, money-saving blog idea I had, we had a huge advantage. Because blogs were still pretty new and very few frugal blogs existed, I had a wide-open field when it came to a website name. My husband and I spent a few weeks tossing around many different ideas. We finally landed on MoneySavingMom.com after much deliberation. We let the idea sit for a few days to make sure that we loved it; it turns out we still did, so we went with it.

Eight years later, we still love the name and never would have dreamed how strong the brand name would be. In fact, it cracked me up at first when people started referring to me as the "Money Saving Mom" because I never started the site thinking that the name referred to me. I just thought it was the perfect way to define my mission—to help moms save money. But now that most people know me by "Money Saving Mom" versus my actual name, I've finally resorted to owning it.

When you land a few names that may work well, check to see if the domain names (the .com website addresses) are available to purchase before jumping ahead and settling on any one name. Many, many domain names are already in use or have been purchased by someone who is hoping to resell them at a higher price. You can search to see if the domain name is available to purchase on DomainsBot.com.

Even if you are planning to have a local, brick-and-mortar business, it's always a good practice to have a website—even if it's just a simple, one-page site advertising your services. We are such an online, internet-driven society that you could miss significant marketing opportunities and exposure by not setting up a website.

When you decide on your name, purchase and set up all variations of that name online. For instance, we own MoneySavingMom .com, MoneySavingMom.net, and MoneySavingMom.org. However, while I did set up Twitter and Facebook profiles early in the game, I waited to jump on the Pinterest and Instagram bandwagons. As

a result, @moneysavingmom on Instagram and Pinterest.com/
MoneySavingMom was already taken, so I had to use @themoney
savingmom on Instagram and Pinterest.com/msmblog.

Marketing

A few months ago, I was getting my hair done at a salon I had never
been to before. The stylist and I started chatting away like old friends.
In our conversation I learned she was also the owner of the salon.

As we shared stories about running our own businesses, she
said something that absolutely shocked me. When asked about
how she drums up business for her hair salon, this woman replied,
"Instagram!" I couldn't believe it! Especially because, up until then,
I'd never heard of any brick-and-mortar business using Instagram
for effective marketing. She shared with me how every day she posts
pictures of before and after haircuts and color as well as formal updo
hairstyles she has done. She tags these pictures with hashtags that
include the city where the hair salon is located. While this business
owner's shop doesn't have what many would consider a large following on Instagram, these pictures generate a lot of likes, attention,
and, most importantly, new clientele.

I was immediately inspired to re-evaluate my own strategies
when it came to Instagram. I realized I had never even considered
using hashtags or finding creative ways to build my brand on that
social media site. You better believe I started posting more often,
using relevant hashtags. The results were outstanding. I was amazed
at how many new followers I gained in just a few months from putting a little effort into Instagram! It goes to show that there are many,
many creative ways to build your brand online and offline.

Think about your business. How do you plan on acquiring

customers? How will you promote your products or services? How will you create awareness around your brand, your value?

I want to encourage you to start by exploring every free option you can come up with before investing a lot of money into paid advertising. Over the years, I've spent very little on paid advertising. It's not been a priority for me when there are so many fantastic free options that work well.

Offer try-it-for-free services. If your business is such that you could offer free consultations or samples (whether music lessons, personal training sessions, or free tastings of your delectable goodies at local supermarkets), this is a great way to build up a clientele. Create parameters for what free means and what it entails so you don't waste too much of your time and effort (and end up losing money in the long run). For example, if your business is tutoring high school students, you can offer a first-time lesson at no cost but charge for future sessions. If you sell skincare, offer sample-sized products for your customers to try for free but charge for full-size quantities. Also, be sure to offer a special discount after the freebie to encourage the potential client or customer to hire you or purchase more of your products.

Tawra from LivingOnADime.com wrote,

> The best thing we have learned about marketing is don't be stingy! When we self-published our cookbook *Dining on a Dime* we gave away hundreds of copies for review. Yes, we had to pay for the shipping and the books, but the free advertising from it was worth much more than we could have ever paid for!

Encourage word of mouth. Once you've built up a small customer base, encourage your customers to spread the word. You can even reward them for doing so by offering a discount coupon or a freebie if they are willing to share about your business with others.

Annaliese has taught music lessons for more than fifteen years. She has offered reduced rates or even free lessons to children in financial need. The very families she has helped have graciously recommended her as a teacher to others and this has resulted in many new students.

Cross-promote other businesses. You can drum up a lot of business by developing relationships, helping other people out, and forging mutually beneficial agreements with other companies. For instance, if you bake and sell wedding cakes, you can network with wedding dress boutiques, tuxedo shops, florists, and wedding photographers. Offer to share their contact information and business cards with your potential clients and ask them to do the same.

Nicole is the president and founder of the Baby Sleep Site (BabySleepSite.com). She offers some great advice based on her many years as a business owner.

I've worked hard to forge partnerships with companies that also cater to moms, and this has yielded great results—it's been a solid, reliable way to drive new traffic to our site, but even more, it has resulted in some strong relationships that have paid off over time. For example, I have a small network of bloggers that I love, and our relationships are so solid now that if I have a new product launch coming up, or if I think it's time to host a giveaway, I can usually just say the word, and they're happy to help (and vice versa, of course!). I see partnering with other like-minded companies as a long-term marketing strategy—while it might not pay huge dividends in terms of additional traffic or increased sale volume right away, it pays off consistently over time, as both businesses grow.

Use social media. When I first started blogging and running an online business, social media didn't exist. Today, it's one of the easiest and most effective options for new businesses to grow. It's an ever-changing market, but I encourage you to hop online, start exploring social media, and find people in your similar niche who are successful. Analyze what they are doing and determine how you could take their ideas and make them work for your business model.

Don't just pay attention to people who are in a similar niche, though. I also get inspired by those who are far, far outside my niche, whether famous musicians who stay grounded and true to their roots, philanthropists doing great things around the world, and anyone who risks and commits to see a dream come true.

When it comes to social media, put the most time and effort into where you see the most traffic, attention, or response. If Twitter posts are pulling in customers, focus on that outlet. If Pinterest creates more chatter than Facebook, keep plugging away there. Work whatever marketing strategies work until they stop working.

Ella and her husband run a small used-car dealership. She is responsible for advertising and has managed to do a great job for next to nothing. She says:

> I built us a very inexpensive website that gets us 70 to 80 hits a week. Not tons, but not bad for such a small-town business. I post pictures of all of our cars on Facebook, put some car listings on Craigslist (we are very picky now as they charge $5 per car listing), and all listings go on Nex-Tech, a local Midwest

classifieds site that charges only $3 per month and 50 cents per listing. I make sure I answer all e-mails and update our listings a few times a week. It works for us!

Nicole of the Baby Sleep Site also offers,

Create branded content for Pinterest—this is so easy to do. You don't even need Photoshop skills—my team uses Pixlr.com and PicMonkey.com to create our branded content (both are online tools that are super easy to use). We started creating pretty, branded pictures to accompany our blog articles, and we've found that this has helped increase Facebook sharing of our blog articles, not to mention getting many more people to share our content on Pinterest than we usually would have. This is a really easy, low-threshold (and free!) way to increase your reach.

Networking

Joyce owns a lawn care company and says that through joining a local networking group, she is able to share with other business owners the "why" and "how" of her company. She has formed relationships with the people in this group, and they have given her many referrals over the years. She also says that it has been a great source of encouragement and information about growing a business.

Building relationships with other bloggers, entrepreneurs, and business owners is a great way to not only learn much but also open up doors for networking. Let me be clear: networking in my mind is not about building relationships with people because of what they can do for you. To me, it's focusing on giving to others.

When I first started out, I didn't have much to offer others. I didn't have many customers, I hardly had any traffic, and I knew very little. But I was determined and eager to learn.

I looked for opportunities to develop relationships with others and did what I could to encourage them. I joined Yahoo! Groups on entrepreneurialism and met a lot of amazing and inspiring folks through these groups. I participated in some great discussions that led to friendships forged outside the group. Not only did these people willingly answer my many questions but some of them even offered to promote my business to their customer base, often giving me a short mention in their e-mail newsletter or allowing me to write an article for their site or e-mail newsletter. Even now, I am amazed at their willingness to promote me, a blogger just starting out, with nothing in return! As I look back, I know their kindness played a big part in not only encouraging me to keep going in my entrepreneurial journey but also helping others discover my site. Some of the same people who stumbled upon MoneySavingMom.com years ago are still loyal readers today!

As my site has grown, I have committed to pass on what those folks did for me by helping to promote others whenever it's a good fit for my audience. This is one of my favorite parts of blogging: getting to introduce my readers to other amazing friends, colleagues, blogs, sites, products, and other resources I find helpful.

Just last week, a blogging colleague sent me a lovely thank-you e-mail. A woman who had been reading her blog for years through my recommendation had approached her in church. She was so excited to meet a loyal reader and just as excited that I had referred her site.

I love celebrating others, especially by being able to promote them. I view my blog as a sort of hub where people gather with questions and I point them in the direction of other blogs and resources that will benefit them and their family's particular needs. I can't be all things to all people, but I can do my best to help readers find a good fit for their particular situation or answers to the questions I am unable to answer.

Unfortunately, because I have a large platform online, I've experienced many uncomfortable situations where people act interested in becoming my friend but I soon find out it's only a front to get something from me. Shortly after meeting me (and without investing in a relationship), they ask me to link to them, promote them, endorse their book, introduce them to other people, put in a good word for them—I could go on and on. I know many people who have used my name, purporting a relationship that didn't exist, just to get their foot in the door with other companies or people. Trust me, there are much, much better ways to grow your business than using others as a step stool.

This is why I've become a big believer in focusing your efforts on giving to others without expectation of return. Find people doing a great thing and encourage, endorse, and do all you can to celebrate them. Be genuine and have zero expectations. Oftentimes, these sincere relationships result in some cool opportunities, but because you've started them without any expectations, you won't face disappointment or hurt even if nothing ever comes of it.

I think there is a great need for us to be less competitive and more celebratory. Life is much more fun when we celebrate people anyway! I have also found that when someone celebrates me, it makes me want to celebrate that person even more. Plus, it shows that he or she is a true friend.

Not too long ago, I attended a conference sponsored by a well-known author and speaker. At the end of the event, I reached out to this woman on Twitter just to let her know that I appreciated her and would be happy to pray or do anything for her that I could.

I was thrilled when she responded. We had a few interactions via text and a phone call. I loved being able to encourage her. While I was hopeful that I could forge at least an ongoing acquaintance with her, I didn't have any expectations beyond that.

A few weeks later, she asked if I would be willing to partner with her on a project. I was floored and honored because her request was so unexpected. In one of our conversations, she mentioned how she was hounded by people who wanted her to do this or that for them and how she struggled with having to say no quite often.

We continued to talk for a bit and finally, curiosity got the best of me. I asked her point blank, "Why did you ask me to partner with you on this project? You don't know me very well and there are so many others who are much more qualified to work with you in this capacity. Why me?"

Her response surprised me! She said,

Crystal, with all the requests I get, I never even consider partnering with someone if they haven't first built a relationship with me. If a stranger or someone I barely know asks for a favor, I never say yes. But if someone has taken time to invest in and build a relationship with me, I will not only seriously consider their requests, I will also actively look for ways we can work together.

You spent money and invested time of your own volition to attend my conference, and you didn't ask for anything from me. Because of that, I could tell that you were someone I wanted to invest in and partner with.

She was right. I attended that conference solely to learn how to be a better speaker and writer. But by investing my time and money, I communicated to her through my actions that I wasn't out for a favor. I'm so grateful that not only have I partnered with this amazing woman on multiple projects but, more importantly, she has become a friend and wise mentor.

You can never be too generous. Think about the people in your life who have encouraged you or given you valuable advice. Return the favor by doing the same for someone else. It is so satisfying to help people, especially when they are working hard and not expecting someone to spoon-feed them or pave their way to success.

Sometimes All It Takes Is Showing Up and Giving Your All

If this is your first time starting a business, you may feel a bit intimidated or even scared. Any new venture comes with its share of fear. You may wonder,

"Will this idea even lift off the ground?"
"Is the market big enough for my product?"
"Can I juggle my business and my life?"
"Can I compete with similar services available?"

While in chapter 7 I'm going to talk in-depth about the fears of risk and failure that hold some people back from pursuing ways to earn income, I want to encourage you that fear is normal. I also want to commend you for being brave enough to try something new to better your life and the lives of those around you.

Recently, I was asked to be the keynote speaker at the Flame Fest

Ball (an event sponsored by FirefighterWife.com, an organization that strengthens and supports wives and their firefighter husbands). I was excited about this event—and especially excited to get dressed up fancy and speak at a ball, of all things! As I rode the elevator down to the hotel lobby, I felt confident (and a bit like Cinderella).

And then I actually stepped foot in the ballroom.

As my eyes gazed over the many couples dressed in their finest, my former confidence disintegrated.

I gulped. What did I have to offer these incredible folks? All around me sat strong and muscular men who willingly risk their lives fighting fires. Next to their sides were equally strong women who endure long days and lonely nights while their firefighter husbands are on duty.

I looked at the strength and courage represented in the room and felt very small. Who was I to stand on stage delivering a message of hope to them? After all, I'm a girl who struggles with anxiety. What do I really know about courage?

But then I remembered . . . sometimes courage is just showing up.

I had a choice in that moment: I could choose to be swallowed up by fear and self-doubt, or I could choose to give it my all, praying that the words I shared would be impactful to those in the audience.

As I got mic'd up, I made a decision to give my all. I left the feelings of fear and insecurity behind, asked God to fill me with courage, and then stood behind the podium, owning this amazing opportunity. When I walked off stage, I knew that while I may not have given the most eloquent talk, I had given it my all.

Fear cripples. It suffocates the life from you. It keeps you from even trying. It whispers things in your ear like, "You're not good enough." "You're not qualified enough." "You're a failure."

But hear me on this: you can push fear away and assert your way toward courage by just showing up and giving your all.

This may mean simply waking up in the morning and doing one thing to move your business forward. Like reading two chapters from a book that teaches how to design a captivating website. Or committing to writing a blog post every day. Or making an appointment with that CEO to get marketing advice. Or tackling your business plan, one goal, one action item, at a time.

Whatever you have to do, show up and give it your all. The rest will follow.

5

Expand Your Thinking,
Expand Your Wallet

If opportunity doesn't knock, build a door.

—MILTON BERLE

I WELL REMEMBER AT ABOUT AGE FIVE SITTING AT A LITTLE kid's card table and selling lemonade for twenty-five cents per Dixie cup at our neighborhood yard sale. For days, I had plotted out the logistics of how I was going to set up my stand, how much I was going to charge, and my goals for how much I wanted to earn. Yes, I suppose you could say the entrepreneurial bug bit me fairly early!

As I got older, I often made my parents listen to many a presentation for my wild and crazy money-making business ventures—like the time I was so sure that I had a killer business idea making handmade cards. Aware that my business idea was quite flawed (I didn't have anywhere to market it, the cards took a long time to make, and

I'm pretty sure that anyone who bought them would only buy them out of pity for me!), my parents gently persuaded me to pursue a different idea.

When I was around eleven, I started helping my older sister with some babysitting jobs. I loved watching kids and found great fulfillment in working hard and helping other people. I did most of this babysitting for free, because I wanted to help the families out and because my parents encouraged me to invest my time and effort into developing a servant's heart.

As I proved to be a hard worker, job opportunities started coming my way. By the time I was fifteen, I was waitressing once a week, teaching violin to at least fifteen students each week, and working as a mother's helper for a few different families. I loved the variety of my life, the challenges each job presented, and being able to have money to pay for items I needed, to give to causes I believed in, and to put into savings.

As I entered my senior year in high school, I considered going to college and ultimately decided against it; my life was so full and enjoyable working multiple part-time jobs. For the next few years and into my first year of marriage, I kept pace. It was tiring, but exhilarating. And I wouldn't trade those years for anything.

When Jesse and I were going through our lean years early in our marriage, I did extensive research online looking into any and every possible way I could earn income from home. The more I researched, the more convinced I became that I needed to change my mind-set about earning an income. Though I made decent money at my various side jobs, the income was dependent upon how much I worked. The more hours I worked, the more money I earned; if I didn't work, I didn't earn money. It didn't take a genius to figure out the only way to get ahead financially with this current method of income-earning ideas would be to work more hours—provided I could find work to do. But I didn't want to work longer hours.

In the course of my research I learned about "residual income," or "passive income." What this means is investing time, energy, and hard work into a project that will provide ongoing future income, without the continual need to work as long or as hard as you initially did. This discovery was mind-blowing. It was almost like earning money without working at all. And it sounded a little too good to be true. Thankfully, it wasn't. As I further explored this concept, I realized this was exactly what I needed to aim for.

I set foot into the new world of residual income by writing and selling e-books and printed booklets through my website. Printed booklets took more time to produce than e-books and produced a much lower profit margin since I had to invest in physical materials. E-books, on the other hand, could be an automated source of income.

In the beginning, I rarely made more than $5 per day selling e-books. But it was a start. And because it only required a one-time up-front investment of time, I quickly realized that making an automated $30 to $50 per week every week for almost zero work (except for the occasional customer service e-mail) was nothing to sneeze at—especially because the initial e-book usually only took me ten hours to create. Over time, as my customer base grew and I improved my products and marketing, I was making a guaranteed $400 to $500 per month off of e-books. On the months I produced a new e-book or put together some sort of package special, I sometimes made twice that amount! See? It really can pay to think outside the box and try new things!

Meredith, one of my blog followers, believes residual income to be key in acquiring financial freedom. She writes,

My husband has a full-time job as an IT manager, but he also owns his own company on the side that does computer programming. He's assembled a team of low-cost programmers, and now all he does is find work to give to the programmers, as well as manage his team. He charges his clients for every hour worked, and he takes a percentage of that fee for each hour. His hourly cut isn't huge, but it adds up, and it's very low stress since someone else is doing the work.

Any time a song is played on the radio, the writer gets paid a particular amount of money. This is another example of residual income. While the songwriter took however long to create the piece of music, once it's recorded and produced in the studio he or she gets a piece of the action for any airtime.

Now, while writing a hit single may not be something you see happening in the near future, there are so many other ways to create residual income, including the following:

- Write an e-book and sell it on Amazon. The onetime up-front investment of time can result in a stream of income month after month.
- Produce an online course on a subject you are knowledgeable about.
- Start a blog and add sidebar ads and affiliate links. While you'll need to update your blog at least somewhat regularly

to see passive income, this is a great way to make money from writing if you love to write.

- Buy a residential home or commercial building and lease or rent out the property.
- Open a savings or investment portfolio that earns interest.
- Create how-to videos and upload them to your channel on YouTube. When you reach a certain number of views, YouTube will pay you a small amount for each view if you add advertisements to your videos.
- Take beautiful pictures and sell the rights to a stock photography site like Dreamstime or Shutterstock.
- Create a mobile app or game and sell it in the Apple store or on Amazon.

Since your time is valuable, you might as well make the most of it by looking for ways to set up residual income streams. Best of all, if you lose your primary source of income, these avenues provide you with financial backup.

One of my blog readers shared with me how she turned her skills into a successful business that ultimately generated additional residual income. When Shelley got married seventeen years ago, she inherited a really ugly couch in the process of merging furniture with her husband. Determined to transform the eyesore into something cute, she purchased some fabric and a pattern to make a slipcover. Much to her disappointment, the fit and pattern didn't work well and she still hated the look of the redesigned couch. But because her budget was tight, Shelley resigned to creating a bit more of an aesthetically pleasing look by making some cushions.

A year later, after moving into a new house, Shelley headed over to a local thrift store and picked up a chair she determined to make a better slipcover for. She read some books on the subject and felt better equipped to make a custom slipcover that didn't just fit well but also looked great. She measured, cut, fit, and designed fabric for the chair and fell in love with the new look. Shelley writes,

> My friends and family loved the slipcover and started asking me to slipcover their furniture. In the meantime I got pregnant with my first child. I told my husband that when we had babies I would stay home and make slipcovers. He laughed (in a good-hearted way) but I was serious. After my baby was born, I had to continue part-time work at Bath & Body Works, but got my first "real" client three months later.

Shelley continued making one or two slipcovers a month upon request. By the time her baby was a year old, business was booming. Not only did she have the income and resources to quit her part-time job, the money she brought in eventually allowed her family to get out of debt and pay off a finished basement, two cars, and even her house. Wow! But that's not all. Here's how Shelley took her business further to generate residual income.

> After we became debt-free, I turned some of my business into an online store where I sell tutorials (slipcover DVD, pillow e-book, and advanced slipcover guide) from my blog. This generates a nice supplemental income ($1,000/month average) that I don't have to work so hard for. Easy money is what I like to call it (after the initial work is done).

I am amazed how a decision to turn something ugly into something beautiful for her home not only transformed into a profitable business but through thinking bigger also provided additional income streams. In the following pages, I've provided examples of how to make extra and ongoing money this way. I'm sharing brief descriptions in each category, mainly to get your wheels turning. If something interests you, hop online and do more thorough research to see if it's an option that would work for you.

E-books

In recent years, with the advent of e-readers and the ease of being able to download e-books from Amazon to your personal device, the publication of e-books has increased tremendously. This opens the door for writers or those who have extensive knowledge in a particular area to get their message and insight out to the masses.

This is good news for many of us. If you have a reputation as an "expert," whether it's cooking gourmet meals in thirty minutes, decorating your house for the holidays on a small budget, or implementing an active and healthy family lifestyle in an unhealthy world, one way to generate income is to write and sell an e-book.

Start teaching people for free (through local or online classes, workshops, or blogging) and develop a reputation as an "expert" to generate excitement for others to buy your materials. Once you create your e-book, you can sell it on Amazon or as a PDF download on your website. I recommend hiring someone like FiveJsDesign.com to set it up for you. It will cost a few hundred dollars but will save you a lot of hassle and create a more professional and refined product than you probably would make on your own.

Real Estate

After Jesse and I hit our huge goal of paying cash for our first house in 2011, we began talking about our next savings goal. My husband has always been interested in real estate and hinted about the possibility of investing in a piece of property or a house. A few conversations and much thought later, we agreed it was a great way to add residual income. After spending countless hours listening to podcasts and reading articles and books about rental property ownership and researching the best areas to invest and the best price range to shoot for, Jesse compiled and presented his findings to me. Together we decided upon a goal for rental house savings.

Over the course of the next year, we threw everything extra we could squeeze out of our irregular business income into our rental house savings. By setting a goal, working toward it, and sticking with our budget each month, we were able to contribute more than we expected. It took us a number of months to find a house that was in the area, price range, and condition we wanted, but persistence paid off! In 2013, we bought our first rental house with cash.

We use a rental management company instead of managing it ourselves, and we have found the partnership to be well worth the 8 percent monthly fee. We've had two different renters in our rental house and so far, pretty good experiences with both. Best of all, we've made a good profit every month, even considering the typical costs involved with occasional repairs and maintenance that come with house ownership.

We are now saving up for a second rental house and diligently researching what area we should purchase in. Our dream is to one day earn more from residual income than we do from our business incomes—not only so we can give more generously but also to provide some space to take new directions with our businesses.

Jennifer, a grandma of two, says,

> I have had rental property for years now. I currently have three units that I rent. While it can be a real pain sometimes when you are between renters or have to deal with someone that doesn't pay on time, it has been a great source of residual income for me since I can't really "work" another job. It's also a great learning opportunity and example for your kids.

Direct Sales

Revenue from the $30 billion direct sales channel has been steadily increasing, up 0.8 percent in 2010, 4.6 percent in 2011, and 5.9 percent in 2012. And for the right personality, it can be a great way to set up a successful business—with the potential for a lot of residual income from sales of those on your team.

Exercise caution when considering direct sales. I have seen women spend a lot of money and energy trying to get a direct sales company started only to end up frustrated, having lost money, and getting themselves into many awkward situations with friends who felt pressured into buying products. Research the company and find out exactly what is required. For example, how much is the starter kit? What is the minimum amount of sales you must achieve each month to remain active? Do you need a certain number of people to sign up under you? Do you have to recruit other salespeople?

To have the most success in direct sales, I highly recommend that you are passionate about the product you sell, have a wide social

network, are a go-getter, and always look for innovative ways to market and sell your products. Being a person who is fairly organized and
someone who has the ability to highly motivate your team of recruits
will also be a great asset.

I have never personally been involved in direct sales, but I know
some women who have been very successful in direct sales. One of
those women is my friend Joy. I asked her if she'd share some of her
story and experience with direct sales. Here's what she said:

I started in direct sales at the age of sixteen, working for Jewels
by Park Lane. Personally, I found that it was a great opportunity.
I usually made $100 to $300 or more for a few hours of work
(an evening party). Plus, I won all-expenses-paid trips to many
fun places, including Germany, Austria, Aruba, Greece, and
Bermuda. Because I sold jewelry, I earned a lot of free jewelry
that I wore almost every single day.

One important thing to remember when you're considering direct sales is this: you are selling a product. If you are
uncomfortable with selling things, you might think twice about
direct sales.

In the jewelry business, we always said, "The jewelry sells
itself." On one hand, that was true. I wore the jewelry every day
(I still do!) and people often stopped me to compliment me on it.
I would tell them where I got it and how they could purchase it
if they were interested. In most cases, they would give me their
contact info. But, that's where the "sells itself" ended. It was up
to me to actually make that contact and see the sale through to
completion.

Another thing to consider is that direct sales often happens in the evenings. You will be gone a few evenings a week to home parties or shows. Working that time of day doesn't work for everyone. On the other hand, it allows you to be home in the day, so if you have small children, this can also be a plus.

Here are some things to consider before going into direct sales:

1. **Choose a company that actually gives you a paycheck.** Some companies let you buy product at a discount and then sell it at full price. The extra money you make you get to keep. In my opinion, this isn't the best way to grow a real business.

2. **Choose a company with a history of honesty and integrity.** The company I worked with, Jewels by Park Lane, has been family owned for sixty years and is completely debt-free. I watched how they treated their people and liked their ethics, both business and personal.

3. **Choose a company that pays you well.** Park Lane starts people out at 30 percent commission. That is on the high side; most direct sales companies start at 20 to 25 percent. Often, the real money to be made is in recruiting and building a team—this is where it gets exciting. Not only does your income go up but you get to teach, train, and encourage other women to be successful. This is a lot of work, but it can be very rewarding.

4. **Choose a company that requires very little money up front.** When I started selling Park Lane, I got $1,000 of jewelry samples to wear and show for ninety-nine dollars. I also started making commission right away. If a company is going to ask you to spend hundreds or thousands of dollars to get started, I would consider a different product.

Direct sales is no longer my full-time job, but in my current business, I owe much of my success to my time in direct sales. I learned how to speak in front of a group, work with people from all different walks of life, train teams of people for excellence, and about the power of recognition and generosity in the lives of others.

Blogging

One of the questions most often e-mailed to me is, "How do you make money blogging?"

The short answer is: it's easier and harder than you may think. It's easy because it requires very little cash outlay up front, you don't need a degree or certification, the field is wide open, and the profit margins are high. On the other hand, setting up a successful blog that makes a part-time or full-time income will only be the result of massive amounts of effort, determination, consistency, and perseverance.

When I started MoneySavingMom.com, I had a huge advantage because I already had a mommy blog that was generating three thousand to five thousand page views per day. In addition, blogging was still pretty new so there weren't as many amazing blogs out there like there are today.

There is so much valuable information you can learn online if you're interested in setting up a successful money-making blog. Below are a few of the most important things to keep in mind:

Pick a great name for your blog. As I mentioned in chapter 4, your blog's name is your brand. The blog name should encompass your blog's mission and clearly articulate its purpose. Don't hurry through the process of picking a name. This is a big deal. You want to make sure you love the name now and think you will love it for years to come.

Produce consistent, quality content. In a market that is already saturated, fresh and unique voices and approaches are those that will stand head and shoulders above the rest. How are you going to be different from all the other bloggers in your niche? If you don't think you could write three posts per week for the next two years on your particular blog topic, you need to talk about something else. Also, people visit a blog more often if they know they can count on it being updated regularly. Commit to posting consistently at least three times each week and you'll be well on your way to building your readership.

Create a community. If you want to build your readership, you need to be there for your readers. Don't just write a post and then disappear and let readers talk amongst themselves in the comments. Respond to questions asked and interact with your readers on a regular basis. In fact, when you first start out, you might try to respond to all comments. It makes people feel a part of a community and encourages them to stick around. Listen to your readers: ask for their advice, welcome their input, and let them know how much you appreciate them.

Don't just connect with readers. Find other bloggers to bounce ideas around, keep each other accountable, and share new things you're learning or experimenting with. These friendships can be invaluable—and it's also nice to spend time with people who "get" what this whole blogging thing is about! Partner with others blogs to create series, raise awareness about issues you care about, and guest post on one another's blogs. Always look for ways to join forces with other bloggers in a way that will benefit your readers—and theirs, as well.

For step-by-step details on how to set up a blog and make money blogging, visit MoneySavingMom.com/make-money-blogging. I also highly recommend that you read *How to Blog for Profit Without Selling Your Soul* by Ruth Soukup.

Remember: It may be a few months (or more!) before you ever see a penny from the hours of labor invested into your blog. Keep testing things out, tweaking your approaches, and learning what works for your audience.

And Many, Many More

I love the friends I've made and the people I've met through my blog and other social media channels. They inspire me by their insight and passion to help others in our web community; they also amaze me by the opportunities they have intentionally created to make a difference in their finances and the lives of others. I am truly blown away by how many different ideas there are to provide financially for you and your household outside of the traditional 8:00 to 5:00 job.

Residual income is just one way to earn money. Let me assure you, there are so many other options to consider. Below are the stories of women who have believed in themselves enough to do something to reach their goal of financial freedom. I hope these testimonies encourage you to see the possibilities.

Keep in mind that every job or at-home business is unique. Each one comes with its own set of challenges, hours, requirements, skills, and earning potential. And as I've said earlier, just because something works for one person doesn't necessarily mean it will work in the same way for you.

Buy It, Make It, Sell It

Are you crafty? Can you sew? Can you build or upholster furniture? Do you have a knack for finding high-quality items for low prices at thrift or consignment shops? Do you have a bunch of furnishings or other home items you need to get rid of?

Consider selling items you make or buy on the cheap on sites like eBay, Craigslist, or Etsy, which require little to no up-front costs. One of my blog readers contracted with a local department store to buy their end-of-season shoes at super low prices and then she sells them on eBay for a nice profit.

Sarah, another blog reader, recently opened an Etsy store, the Amateur Naturalist, which sells terrarium kits and accessories. Though it's relatively new, the response has been positive. While Etsy is a hot spot for at-home businesses and its competitive marketplace can turn off potential business owners, Sarah has great advice on how to make your business or idea stand out. She writes,

> I've learned a lot about Etsy SEO (optimizing your product or store to come up better in searches) and I believe that has really helped people find our products. Also, I recommend focusing on something that makes your products unique, and finding some niche to help you stand out. Great photos are definitely key on Etsy. We had a photographer friend help us with a lot of ours.
>
> If you decide to sell online, here are some tips:

- post good photos
- use accurate descriptions
- list a reasonable price
- respond to inquiries in a timely manner

Earn While You Burn

Deedee teaches fitness classes at a local gym. She says,

> Part of my employment is that I get a free membership. You may also be able to negotiate a membership for your husband or other family members at some gyms. While I may not get paid that much, it is totally worth the membership (about $40/month) and it makes me go to the gym.

While Deedee chose a more traditional route, you may consider the possibilities of being a personal trainer or fitness instructor where you can either work out of a home gym or "freelance" at multiple fitness centers. You may need appropriate certification, but this type of work can be flexible and may even include child care. Also, it's a great way to stay in shape (and get paid at the same time!).

Misty wrote,

> I'm a water exercise instructor at our local Y. The Y actually pays me to get my CPR, first aid, and other safety certifications. My whole family enjoys the free family membership, along with discounts on summer camps and private lessons.

People and Pet Care

Love people? Babies? Kids? Animals? Consider taking care of someone or something.

If you love animals, seek jobs as a pet sitter or a dog walker in your neighborhood. I know plenty of people who own dogs and are looking for an alternative to a kennel when they're going out of town. Same with folks who work full-time; many of them would love to have someone take their beloved furry pets for a walk or give them some love in the middle of the day.

Janice, an avid dog lover, loves her doggie-sitting business. Here is what she has to say,

> I get to have a dog or three for a day or two weeks! My kids love it, I love it, and it closes the gap for our finances. I pre-screen the dogs through a "meet and greet" so I can see if it's the right fit. I take breaks when I need to, I get to stay home with the kids, and I get to love on dogs. I've made my business an LLC, although you don't have to. I heard about it through a site called DogVacay.com. I'm insured through them, marketed through them, and am thankful for their background support.

What about kids? If you have small children, you probably understand the challenge of finding affordable and trustworthy child care. Think about offering babysitting services to a friend or someone in your community or even opening a day care in your home. While the latter may require state licensing, depending on the number of children you watch, it may be a great option.

Pam has been a child care provider in her home for the last six years. It's a tough job, but she enjoys it and the perks that come with it. She writes,

> It is hard work but you are allowed to be at home with your children, which is a bonus. I am able to contribute to our income and I am happy doing what I love, teaching and taking care of children. This job is NOT for everyone. I am open 6am to 6pm, which makes for a long day.

You may also consider house-sitting for people who are on vacation or watching a friend's elderly parent or grandparent for a few hours a day.

Don't Lose Your Skills, Use Them

I know so many mothers who have college degrees, certifications, and unique training that have collected dust over the years. Certainly, many of these women have dedicated their lives to parenting and have no intention or desire of resurrecting a career or vocation that has thoughtfully been laid to rest.

And yet, there are women who want or need to make some money to improve or simply sustain their financial situation. If this applies to you, you can follow Cathy's lead and reclaim your niche in a particular area or field in which you are experienced.

She writes,

> I've been running my web and print marketing design business from my home office for the last 5 years (CanopyWebDesign .com). Even though I went back to work full-time outside the home a year ago, I've kept my design business going for a few clients. This keeps my skills current in case I need them again down the road. I also just love working with clients, especially when I've come up with a design that captures exactly what they're looking for.

Whether you have worked as a graphic designer, executive, attorney, teacher, or nurse, consider translating your skills into a side job. Are you good at something that can be done electronically, like editing a manuscript, updating a website, or doing research? Check out freelance sites like Guru.com and upwork.com. Did you love English class in high school? Maybe you were a teacher before you decided to stay home with your kids. Offer tutoring to local students or at a community center. Make connections with your child's teachers and the PTA.

Attention: Inventors Wanted

Hundreds of thousands of inventions have proved useful, some on which we base our very survival. And, sure, some inventions are downright silly yet have earned their creators millions of dollars (hello, pet rock, anyone?).

I recently received an e-mail from Jill, who opted to increase her income through an invention, on a shoestring budget no less. At first, she didn't have any ideas. Then, inspiration came in the form of an unexpected death. One of the chickens she raised on her farm had been pecked to death from injuries sustained during mating. While an item known as a "hen saddle" would have protected the chicken's back, she was dissatisfied with existing products. They were too expensive to purchase in bulk, and they needed to be washed all the time.

She began brainstorming with her husband on how they could improve the poultry device. After a year of testing various materials and prototype designs, they created a patent-pending design that was cheaper than any competitor's pricing and required little maintenance.

Guess how much it cost this couple to invent, market, and get feedback from their test designs? Twenty bucks! That's right! They kept advertising costs minimal by advertising on niche chicken and gardening forums, selling on eBay and Etsy, pitching for product reviews (with a giveaway) on popular chicken blogs (yup! They're out there!), and pitching stories featuring their product, story, and business to niche and local media. Since creating this product in 2012, they have sold over ten thousand products and make a decent part-time income. Brilliant!

Do you have an idea you think might work? Jill offers some great tips to would-be inventors:

- Make something that is yours—something that simply isn't on the market. Trying to compete with and undercut an already established competitor will just leave you frustrated.
- Find your niche. What are you interested in? What is your profession? What are your hobbies? Maybe develop an app that does something no other app currently does.
- Have little funding? You can always try crowd-funding sites like Kickstarter.com to help to raise funds. If you have a marketable product, Etsy (handmade items) and eBay are good low-barrier sites to start selling your wares on.
- Keep advertising costs down by writing and pitching unusual stories to the appropriate media. Make sure you know your niche market. Pitching your story to *Forbes* magazine may give you a huge audience but *Forbes* will probably not run your story, nor will their audience necessarily be interested in your invention.
- Protect your idea. If it is something new and different, protect your invention with a patent and save yourself the heartache of someone stealing your product!

Bree, a mom who lives in Punta Gorda, Florida, is another example of someone who came up with a creative invention to make her life as a mom easier. Before marriage, she held high-earning jobs that required her to work long hours. After marrying the love of her life and having her daughter, she knew she didn't want to continue working all the time and, instead, wanted to be able to have plenty of time to spend with her daughter.

Here's her inspiring story:

I knew my previous work habits wouldn't cut it. Spending time together as a family was far more precious and memorable than the big paycheck I'd earn for working long hours. As a result, I committed to developing something that would allow for maximum profits without giving up precious time with my family. Literally minutes later the Mason Muggy was born (MasonMuggy.com).

Sitting at my computer staring at a blank page and sipping coffee from my favorite Mason jar cup, my daughter relentlessly tugging at my pant leg and begging to use my cup, the *aha!* moment struck. My young daughter didn't want to use a toddler cup and would only drink from a bottle or whatever cup Mommy was currently using, so I began searching the web for toddler Mason jar cups and found nothing. I realized that if I could find a way to make a toddler Mason jar cup, it could not only be profitable, it could also solve my sippy cup dilemma.

My heart raced with excitement as I called my husband and rambled on about my crazy idea to create a toddler Mason jar cup. To my surprise, he agreed that it was a great idea. That was all I needed to hear. Soon after, a TV commercial caught my attention. It was for a show on the Discovery Channel called *Billy Bob's Gags to Riches*, and they were promoting that they were looking for new inventors of "Redneck" products. I was determined to be on that show! I wrote down the details to contact the company and loaded my daughter into the car. Off we went in search of the items needed to make our first prototype.

A single stop at a big box store, and we had everything we needed for less than $6 to make our first Mason Muggy. We had a working prototype that evening and my daughter was no longer drinking from a bottle! It was SUCCESS on so many levels. I showed it to family and friends and all of the reactions were the same: "Where can we get one?!"

I snapped a few photos of the prototype, drafted up a quick e-mail, and sent it off to the company looking for "Redneck" inventions. Then I pulled up a list of the closest patent attorneys and made an appointment. Eight grueling hours in his office with a toddler later, we had filled our provisional patent, trademarks, and copyrights!

A few short days later, in the midst of changing a dirty diaper, my phone rang. I didn't recognize the number so I let it go to voice mail and went about my mommy duties. It wasn't until several hours later when my husband got home that I remembered to check my voice mail. Standing in the parking lot watching him spin our daughter in circles I started to listen to the message; my eyes flooded with tears, and I literally started jumping for joy. The message was from the Discovery Channel producer, and he was inviting us to Hardin, Illinois, to pitch our idea!

My little Mason jar sippy cup was featured on *Billy Bob's Gags to Riches*, and I was offered a 10 percent licensing deal with Jonah White. The "Billy Bob Mason Jar Sippy Cup" will be hitting some large retailers in just a few months. I still hold the patent, trademarks, and copyrights for the original Mason jar sippy cup (the Mason Muggy). I will be launching a second cup that focuses on our company slogan "Smiles with Every Sip," and adopting a one-for-one business model. For every Mason Muggy sold, we will provide clean drinking water to a child in need.

Fill a Void

Lynn knows one of the challenges of being a working mom is the time you spend shuffling your kids to soccer practice, band club, choir rehearsal, football games, study groups, and a slew of other commitments. So she decided to help fellow mothers by offering her services as a local chauffeur. She drives around older neighborhood kids to their dentist appointments or out-of-town tournaments when their parents are stuck late at work or are double-booked with other children.

Natalie is a stay-at-home mom of two boys. While she implemented many budgeting and money-saving strategies, money was still tight and she wanted to contribute to her family's finances. At the same time, her son was suffering with eczema. Nothing helped, not endless trips to the dermatologist nor countless prescriptive creams and ointments. At her wit's end, she took a holistic approach and purchased balm from a local farmer's market. To Natalie's and her son's amazement (and relief), it worked!

Inspired by this discovery, Natalie began to question her family's past skincare choices and decided to research less toxic and more natural options. She started a company called Nu Natural, a mobile boutique that provides non-toxic, handmade skincare, sourced from artisans and small businesses and sold at affordable prices. Because her business is mobile (similar to a food truck), she is able to keep her overhead low so she can pass on the savings to customers.

I love that not only is Natalie's business a success and helps promote local artisans, many of whom are stay-at-home moms, but she also donates 5 percent of profits to a home in Kenya for pregnant girls. Natalie says,

Before starting Nu Natural, I worked in the non-profit sector for over eight years. When I came up with this business idea, it was imperative that I found a way to give back both locally and globally.

What a great way to make a difference!

Virtual Assistant

Being a virtual assistant is a wonderful choice for an organized stay-at-home mom. I know a woman who ran a business and depended heavily on an employee who lived two time zones away. This virtual assistant handled all kinds of work—phone calls, bookkeeping, website updates. It was a perfect arrangement. The assistant was able to be home with her kids and keep a flexible schedule and the business owner had a wonderful and dependable assistant.

Currently, all of my team members work virtually; most are busy moms who work from home on their own schedules and timetables. They have specific projects to oversee and tasks to complete, but most of them can be done whenever it works best for their schedules. This is such a win-win for me!

With modern technology, there are many possibilities and opportunities to work virtually for other online businesses for those people who are driven, dependable, and detail-oriented. In fact, there is always a shortage of good virtual assistants—it seems that everyone with a great reputation is completely booked and other bloggers and online business owners are constantly coming to me asking if I have any recommendations for them!

One of my blog followers, Brandy, worked in the corporate world for fifteen years. When her third child was born, she determined to stay home until kids were in school full-time. She ran an Internet business, which was flexible but didn't bring in enough income. Then she started a cleaning service, which earned a good amount of income but provided no flexibility with her children. Finally, Brandy became a virtual assistant for a broker in the next state. She works around twenty-five hours a week, which gives her enough supplemental income to provide for her household and enough flexibility to be involved in her children's lives before and after school. She has a great suggestion for women looking to work from home. Brandy suggests,

> Find something that fits your schedule, skills, and what you LIKE to do. Also have a separate office and carve out set hours to work. Don't let your at-home business take over your at-home life.

Check out Lisa Morosky's book, *The Bootstrap VA*, for more information about this field.

Survey Says . . .

I had no idea what I was doing when I signed up for online survey companies. While I discovered that most of them are much more work than they are worth, I don't think they all should be discounted.

Understand that you won't get rich taking surveys and you're probably not going to make any more than ten dollars per hour, if that. But if you're patient, persistent, and thorough, you will definitely earn some money—especially if you sign up with companies that are legitimate and have a good reputation in the online survey world. Taking surveys can be a fun way to add a little additional side income stream—and it's something you can do on your own time.

A few tips:

- Do set up a separate e-mail address for surveys. You will get extra advertisement-type e-mails as a result, so no need to fill up your regular inbox with these.
- Don't take surveys that only enter you into sweepstakes. This is not worth the return on your investment of time.
- Don't get discouraged if it's slow going at first. It takes a little while to learn what types of surveys you enjoy most and which ones are worth the effort. Stick with it and you'll get a much better grasp on where the best return on your investment of time is when it comes to surveys.

Katie has been participating in survey sites for a few years. This year she is on target to make around $900. She writes,

This year was great because I was sent two bras to test, which I got to keep, and I earned $7 for testing them out and giving my feedback. I have also tested shampoo, conditioner, and more. So not only am I earning money, but I am also saving money by not having to buy these products for a while!

Erin sings the praises of UserTesting.com. A typical week will earn her $150–$200. She began a few months ago intending to make enough money to buy her husband an Xbox. At first, she made about fifty dollars a week, which equates to about one test per day, for ten to fifteen minutes. She says,

> The longer you do surveys, and the higher your ranking, the more opportunities you get. I get many more than I can get to at this point, so I've become really picky about the ones I take.

Shop Till You Drop

You've probably seen magazine or web ads that promise you can make hundreds of dollars every month by shopping and going out to eat. And you've probably thought it was too good to be true. I mean c'mon, right?

Well, those advertisements are likely using persuasive language designed to get you to sign up for some overpriced list, which you can find yourself with a little searching online. But, believe it or not, mystery shopping is a legitimate source of income. And in many metropolitan areas, the jobs are plentiful and the pay is decent.

When I experimented with this source of income, I signed up for all of the mystery shopping companies listed at Volition.com. I opened up a separate e-mail account, which was dedicated solely to mystery shopping e-mails. It took me hours to sign up, but the effort paid off as I landed dozens of great mystery shopping jobs over the next two years. I mystery shopped at fast food places, casual dining eateries, high-end restaurants, gas stations, beauty supply stores, pet stores, and even a bowling alley, to name a few. Restaurants were my favorite, as they usually not only reimbursed meals for my husband and me, they also usually paid at least an extra ten dollars for the work involved.

So how much can you make? Well, it depends. Most jobs offer

seven to fifteen dollars (and include some sort of reimbursement as well) for an average of an hour's worth of work. Once you've established yourself with a company, you may be offered jobs that pay twenty to twenty-five dollars per hour, or more. These jobs are typically not offered to newbies.

If this is something you're interested in, be sure to only work with legitimate companies that don't require up-front costs. Check out the MSPA's website (Mystery Shopping Providers Association; MysteryShop.org), which acts as a BBB for mystery shopping.

Also, take the time to thoroughly fill out all applications. And have patience. Over time, you'll likely begin to see quite a number of job opportunities sent to you. Many openings are filled on a first-come, first-served basis, so check your e-mail a few times each day and be quick to respond to those you are interested in.

Just Ask

One of the ways to find opportunities to make money is to simply ask. When you make known to others what you are looking for, you increase your likelihood of someone sharing your need or recommending your services to someone who needs it. Sometimes word of mouth is a better source than searching through online or other want ads.

Brenda is a single mom of four boys who works full-time outside of the home. She's done myriad things to provide for her family—like babysitting, house-sitting, selling Tupperware, and participating in countless consignment sales. She says, "The biggest piece of advice I can give other moms is to let people know you are looking for extra money. I have gotten all of my extra jobs through word of mouth."

Don't be too timid or embarrassed to tell others you need to earn some money. When you are looking for solutions you'll only find them if you open yourself to receiving them. And you'll only be able to do that if you are honest and open with others and tell them what you are looking for. It just might be that your sister knows a neighbor who needs help redecorating her house, or a friend knows someone who is looking for a nanny, or a colleague knows a business owner who needs someone to help with accounting issues.

I hope by now you are encouraged by the possibilities. Whatever your financial situation, know there is hope. Let that hope sink in and sit with you. Surround yourself with positive influences who will encourage and motivate you. Choose to be thankful, even when life feels so overwhelming. Find something—anything—to be thankful for. However small these actions might seem, they are powerful forces. They help you maintain a position to never give up. Things can change; they can get better. When you take small steps in the right direction—from reading books on how to make money, to having a positive attitude, to digging deep for opportunities—you grow as a person. And eventually, your opportunities grow in turn. Let's look at that kind of growth in the next chapter.

6

Growing Your Business

Growth is the great separator between those who
succeed and those who do not. When I see a person
beginning to separate themselves from the pack,
it's almost always due to personal growth.

—JOHN C. MAXWELL

AMY'S MOM AND GRANDMOTHERS TAUGHT HER HOW TO
sew. She can still hear them say, "Why buy it when you can make
it?" As a little girl, she sat with these women, carefully measuring
out beautiful fabric with the hypnotic hum of sewing machines in
the background and transforming shapeless material into beautiful
dresses, costumes, and pillowcases.

As she became an adult, Amy's hobby took a backseat. When
she became pregnant with her first child in 2007, she dusted off
her sewing machine (and her skills) and made burp cloths for her
baby, thanks in part to the high number of free tutorials that floated

around the web. For the next three years, Amy cultivated her creative gift, sewing only for her children. The more she sewed, the better she got. The requests soon poured in from friends and family to sew items for them.

In 2011, Amy started her own Etsy shop, listing only a few things each month, depending on the amount of spare time she had. The business produced small but consistent profit. Two years later, Amy's husband, who was in graduate school at the time, owned a business that started tanking. Their once-stable financial picture crumbled, and they needed extra income immediately just to survive. Amy thought she could possibly contribute to the family budget by increasing her product offerings, improving the photos, and buying more products at a wholesale cost.

So she worked hard to grow her business (GabrielsGoodTidings .com), offering and selling more products than she had ever sold, and was even featured multiple times on daily deal sites. Her first feature was on Jane.com, and she sold out of nearly two hundred items in less than twelve hours! Sales continue to flourish as Amy has since expanded her business, partnering with other sites like Zulily.com and several companies where she offers large quantities of items at wholesale prices. In 2014, Amy's business became her family's primary source of income.

I love reading inspiring success stories like these. While we ought to congratulate Amy on her success, keep in mind, she didn't grow her business in a day. She has had to make sacrifices along the way including saying no often. Amy writes,

> The most important things in my life are my husband and sup-
> porting him through school, my kids and their schooling, and

making sure this business will meet our budget needs each month. Most everything else just falls off my radar screen.

To reach her growth goals, she also enlists the help of her family. Amy is grateful her kids pitch in and help package, stack, and organize products. She also made wise financial business decisions along the way without sacrificing the quality of the products she made.

Once you've established your business, maintained a good pace, and know what you're getting into, it may be time to set your sights higher and start focusing on growth.

Slow, Smart Growth

Growth doesn't come without its share of challenges. If your business expands in a short amount of time and you're not ready for it, something—whether in your business or personal life—will become compromised.

I'm a big believer in slow growth. I think it's much more sustainable over time than fast and quick growth. So aim for a steady and slow upward climb versus a massive jump. Not only is this less overwhelming for you, but it is much easier to sustain financially.

Beth is a work-at-home mom who was on a strict budget after she separated from her husband. He had made some poor financial choices and left her with so much debt she had no choice but to claim bankruptcy. Money was so tight, there were many days Beth wondered how she was going to get food on the table.

In 2010, quickly falling behind on her mortgage, Beth started selling items on eBay while holding down a merchandising job at a local grocery store. When she sprained her ankle and was forced to quit her job, she began doing heavy research on how to make more money selling online. She was part of a Facebook support group of eBay sellers at the time and noticed many of these people talked about selling on Amazon. After two more months of research, she started selling there through Amazon's fulfillment program. She would purchase items for resale from popular retail stores like Walmart and Target and then ship those products to the Amazon warehouse where they would mail the items to customers when they sold. While in some ways her business is similar to selling on eBay, Beth found it to be less labor intensive and more profitable.

Although money was still tight, Beth was able to support her family with her business. Still, she wanted more financial freedom than simply paying the bills and a few extras. As time passed, she partnered with a friend and began consulting, writing books, and teaching others how to sell on Amazon. A year later, those residual sources of income combined bring in more money annually than she and her husband made jointly before they separated.

It took several years for Beth to fully support her family. She told me it would have probably taken less time, however, had she made better decisions and formulated a plan of action. Here's what she has to say in her own words.

I started right before the biggest selling season of the year and I was hoping to make an extra $1,000 a month. I sold almost $50,000 during that time. But because I didn't really know what I was doing, and was woefully unprepared for that amount of business, I made bad buying choices (thinking nothing of spending one hundred dollars on an item that would only profit me twenty dollars), put things on credit (that I was sure would sell and I would pay it off; but they didn't sell for months), and let my desperation over our financial situation direct my decisions instead of allowing the peace of God to rule in my mind and heart.

In January of 2013, due to family and financial circumstances, I basically had to start my business over again. I had some inventory and a little investment money this time, but most of all, I had experience and knowledge that I didn't have the first time around. I now operate *PlayDreamGrow.com* on a 98 percent cash basis. I do have a credit card, but use it sparingly and pay it off within 2 months (or less) when I do use it. Within just a few months, I was making enough profit to support me and my children because I was making better buying choices and relying on my faith, rather than panicking. I still had some lean months, but I was never late on a bill and my kids always had food. It has been growing ever since.

Grow Your Income Ahead of Your Expenses

Before I even begin to give you some pointers for growing your business, I want to stress the importance of handling your finances with wisdom. As I mentioned in chapter 4, you must determine your budget for your business ahead of time.

Pouring thousands of dollars through loans into a business before you can afford it is never a good option. This is why I'm a big advocate of growing your income before you grow your expenses. Don't make purchases or hire employees until you absolutely know you have the wiggle room to afford them in your business budget. A friend of mine who owns her own literary agency budgets in advance a year's salary for any employee she considers hiring. This helps keep her finances in check.

I'm a firm believer in avoiding debt when starting a business. To do so means you'll probably need to make some pretty significant sacrifices in the beginning. You might not have a nice computer or a plush office. In fact, you might start your business on a card table in your living room on a laptop that barely works. It's not ideal, but in the words of Theodore Roosevelt, "Do what you can, with what you have, where you are."[1] Start with what you have and make the most of it until you are in a position to upgrade to something better.

When my husband launched his law firm, he didn't have money to invest in new furniture for his office. So he bought some used pieces from an auction. Sure, it wasn't the sleekest looking law office on the block, but the furniture served its purpose until the firm made enough money for him to budget for new furniture.

When I started building an online business, I couldn't even afford to pay for Internet access. So guess what I did? I got creative! Do you remember those CDs from AOL that came in the mail offering three months of dial-up Internet for free? Well, we signed up! When the trial was almost up, I called to cancel, only AOL wouldn't let me. Instead they gave me another three months for free. This happened over and over again—for almost two years!

I still remember the thrilling day when the business was finally making enough money that I could justify paying for high-speed Internet. It felt surreal. And, boy, did it save me so much more time than dial-up. But for those first two years, it was worth it to plug away on the slow Internet because it was the only price tag we could afford at the time—free!

One of the greatest mistakes people make is throwing a bunch of money at their business in order to build it. Now, there are times this kind of investment can be a good thing, but it's likely you will not have a ton of money when you start out. This is why you must make sure your expenses don't exceed your income. This may seem like basic Budgeting 101, but it's amazing how many people forget that the bottom line is one of the most important things in a business. If you're not making money, you're going to sink—and fast!

I'm very frugal by nature, so I tend to proceed with extreme caution when it comes to business finances. In fact, I'll often wait to hire someone or invest in something until I absolutely, without-a-shadow-of-a-doubt can prove that it will be worth it. It may seem obsessive, but this frugal mentality has served me well. We have worked hard to keep our profit margin high and our costs low. As we add on new expenses, I have to be able to not only justify their value but also determine how we're actively increasing our income in order to pay for the additional expenses.

Remember the story I told in the beginning of chapter 4 about Lizanne Falsetto, the CEO of thinkThin? In 1999, she had raised enough funds to create a small product line, which was sold to her first customer, Whole Foods Market. Refusing to take on any loans to grow her business, she said, "If I didn't have the money for something, I found a way to make it happen that I could afford."[2] To help keep costs low, she also enlisted the help of friends and family. But as the business grew, she began hiring full-time individuals with experience in the food market. There were times her finances restricted her company's ability to grow as quickly as she would have liked. When she couldn't afford to hire new employees, she relied on consultants to fill in the gaps. It wasn't always her first choice, but it got the job done and allowed her to stay out of debt. I admire Lizanne's commitment to using financial wisdom to grow. Clearly, it has paid off.

Always Set Aside Money in Savings

Making an intentional effort to keep our income well ahead of our expenses also has allowed my husband and me to set aside a significant amount of money in our business savings account. Especially as you grow, it's wise to build a strong savings account. Think of this as an "emergency fund" for the business. If an unexpected expense comes up, you have a less-than-stellar month income-wise, or you want to invest in something for your business (like producing a new product, buying more inventory, or hiring a consulting company for a short-term project), you will have enough money set aside that you won't financially stumble or even think about borrowing from somewhere or someone.

Up to this point, we have rarely had to dip into our savings account to pay our regular expenses. However, it brings us great comfort knowing we have a good cushion built up in case something does happen. It's also great to have this so we can invest back into the business, fund the production of a new product, or make a large purchase.

Grow Your Income Possibilities

One of the smartest ways to grow your business is to look for ways to make additional income from things you already have set in place. Think about the business you're in or would like to create. What additional services can you provide that will bring in extra income? For instance, if you mow lawns as a side job, could you also offer trimming services? Or teach a class on how to set up a successful lawn-mowing business?

If you have already written an e-book that has sold well, could you produce and market other people's e-books for them since you already know how to do it yourself? Or offer e-book coaching or consulting services?

Sarah Mae proved herself as a skillful e-book marketer when her e-book, *31 Days to Clean*, brought in over $20,000 in revenue. She took that knowledge and experience and wrote an e-book on how to successfully market an e-book.

Dave Ramsey offered his staff and their friends a weekly class on how to run a successful business and eventually turned it into the EntreLeadership Live Event and the *EntreLeadership* book.

Think of ways to grow and stretch your business outside of what you currently offer.

Don't Put All Your Eggs into One Basket

I first heard of the concept of income diversification when I learned about residual income. The concept of diversifying your income means setting up various income-producing sources, instead of putting all your eggs into one basket and expecting that basket to be your sole source of sustenance.

We realized the beauty of income diversification when Jesse was unemployed when we lived in Kansas City. Since I had spent the two years prior experimenting with ways to earn money from home, we had a cushion to fall back on. It wasn't a very soft cushion, but at least it kept us from crashing and burning.

When people ask me how I make money blogging, most of the time they are quite taken aback when I say, "It's the power of multiple streams of income." My blog earns a significant amount of money every month, but it comes in through dozens of different checks and electronic transfers from dozens of companies. The checks vary a great deal in their amounts, but each check brings in at least a trickle that turns into a steady stream of income to pay my team, cover our business expenses, invest in business projects, and give to causes we believe in, with extra leftover for personal income and savings.

In blogging—as in most businesses—things ebb and flow. Certain things will do really well at certain times of the year. At other times, those same income streams don't do so well. If I were to rely only on sidebar advertising, or product sales, or speaking, or one affiliate program for all of my income, it would be a lot lower than it is. But because I have many profit-earning channels in place, the ebbs and flows balance each other out so that the income is fairly consistent.

It's very important that you're always continuing to look for ways to diversify your income. I was reminded of the importance of this in 2013. For years, blog and affiliate advertising had been the strongest revenue stream on MoneySavingMom.com. I had many different affiliates I was working with, so I felt like I was diversifying enough. But then, a few months before we decided to move to Tennessee, without warning, Kansas changed its laws for those who use affiliate programs. A few of the larger companies we had been working with and earning a hefty paycheck from each month could no longer work with us because of these new laws.

This change happened in a very short time—right before the Christmas season, our highest earning time of the year—and resulted in a loss of thousands of dollars in potential sales from those companies during the especially profitable holiday season. This is why it's so important to focus on diversifying. You never know when one income stream will no longer be as strong because of some sort of change.

If you get multiple money-making ideas going, it's easy to become complacent. Of course, if you land on things that are really working well, don't jump ship. But likewise, don't get stuck in a rut. Constantly challenge yourself to look for new ways to improve and expand so that you maximize the return on your investment of time.

Ask your friends for ideas of ways you could add additional income streams. Pay attention to what your customers are asking for. Watch what other successful people are doing. And just jump out there and try new things.

Grow Your Team

When you are just starting out your business—whether you are selling jewelry, providing music lessons, cleaning houses, or offering graphic design services—don't even consider hiring help right away.

I always encourage budding entrepreneurs to learn all they can about the different aspects of their business. For instance, you may not be a techie, but you should learn the fundamentals of a website (if you have one), how to increase traffic, and how to update it regularly. Sure, it may be easier and save you some time to have someone else do it for you, but that's an extra expense that may not fit into your budget. Not only that, but how can you know someone is a good hire if you don't know how that person's job is supposed to be done—and done well?

When my first book came out, I managed its launch almost entirely single-handedly. My team was still very small at that point and I was a newbie to book launches. I figured it made the best sense to handle things on my own and figure out what worked and what didn't. I invested countless hours and weeks researching and sending and reviewing thousands of e-mails, but my "investment" paid off.

I learned so much on my own that the second time around, I had a solid grasp on effective strategies and guidelines in approaching the launch, what tasks I could handle well myself, and other responsibilities I could delegate to others.

It's no secret that MoneySavingMom.com is a team effort. Today, there are sixteen people who work for the business, all of whom are employed virtually at this time all across the country. But for the first few years, it was just me.

I hired my first team member two and a half years after I created MoneySavingMom.com. I was moving my blog from Typepad to WordPress and needed a person with more tech knowledge to help with the process. I have a basic knowledge of how to fix and tweak websites, but moving thousands and thousands of comments and posts from one place to another was well beyond my scope of limited knowledge. I knew I needed help, but for someone as frugal as I am, hiring someone felt like an extravagant expense. Also, as a recovering control freak, it was hard to think of relinquishing some of my control to someone else.

I am so grateful I pushed through these thoughts and decided to hire Joy from FiveJsDesign.com. She has been worth every penny and so much more. Why? Because not only can she do in fifteen minutes what would take me four hours, but by handing off the graphic design and tech stuff to her, it freed me up to focus more time on things that only I can do.

The success with this first hire inspired me to bring on board a few more people and then a few more. Years later, I woke up one day and realized I was no longer just a solo blogger. I had turned an idea into an actual company with a real team of amazing people. I am so very thankful for each and every person who makes up the

MoneySavingMom.com team. I could not do what I do without their expertise, commitment, and dedication to our vision and goals.

If you are at the place where you can afford to hire an extra pair of hands or eyes, here are some pointers for you:

- Write a detailed job description. Make a list of every responsibility the position entails.
- Have firsthand knowledge into what you expect the hire to do so you can best evaluate his or her performance.
- Start small. Hire on a part-time basis, a few hours a week, before you make the full-time plunge.
- Start slowly. Give your employee or contractor a short-term project so you can assess his or her work on the little things.
- Observe how quickly the person responds to your requests, how well he or she handles constructive criticism, and how well you work together.
- Focus on the hire's character. (Does the person pursue excellence in everything he or she does?)
- Make sure you clearly communicate what success looks like. Share goals and progress.

I go to great lengths to find the right person for the right seat on my team because I know how important it is to have a spirit of unity and cohesiveness as a group. In fact, there are certain positions that I've waited more than a year to fill because I hadn't found the right person yet. I'd rather take my time, observe someone's character, and try out some small projects to make sure a person is the right fit. And I'd much rather have a position unfilled than to have someone filling it who isn't the right man or woman for the job.

Grow as an Individual

In reading Jon Acuff's blog, I learned that in 2012, Dave Ramsey, financial guru and author of multiple *New York Times* bestselling books including the acclaimed *Financial Peace*, celebrated twenty years on the radio. That's a big deal in light of the cutthroat, short shelf life of the radio world. Jon Acuff shared,

> During a Q&A session, someone asked Dave a question. They said, "What was the moment you realized that you had arrived?"
>
> Dave's answer surprised everyone in the crowd. Without missing a beat, he said, "We haven't arrived yet. There's still so much we need to do. We've got a lot of work ahead of us."[3]

Dave Ramsey leads a company of hundreds. He inspires millions through his radio show, books, websites, and courses every single week. Yet, he clearly doesn't feel like he's made it.

I think there's a lesson here for all of us. We should never, ever feel like we've arrived. There are always many more things we can learn, many more ways we can improve, many more ways we can expand our thinking, many more ways we can grow.

If you want to grow your business, you need to grow as an individual. Successful leaders are those who aren't content with the status quo. Here are some ways to continue growing:

Read. Challenge yourself to read at least one new business or leadership book every month from or about people who started successful companies (like S. Truett Cathy, David Greene, Joel Manby, and Sam Walton). Read books that help you develop strong character as a business owner and motivate you to keep reaching for new ideas (such as *What the Most Successful People Do on the Weekend, Developing the Leader Within You,* and *Becoming a Person of Influence*; see the Resources section at the back of the book for more suggestions).

I also encourage you to subscribe to a magazine like *Inc.* or *Fast Company*, follow blogs like *Michael Hyatt* and *Chris LoCurto*, and listen to podcasts like *EntreLeadership* or *Brilliant Business Moms*. On BrilliantBusinessMoms.com, Sarah and Beth Anne interview entrepreneurial moms who are successful in a variety of businesses but also desire to have a healthy work-life balance.

Find a mentor. I've become a firm believer in having mentors in your life. I'm blessed with a husband and two managers who serve as mine. I'm constantly asking Jesse for counsel in sticky or perplexing situations. He is also a great sounding board for new ideas or things I'm considering. My managers, Brian and Joy, have been incredible additions to my team (and my life) in the past two years. I'm honored to have them not only help shape the future of our business but also speak into my life on a weekly basis. Joy and Brian challenge me to dream big, step outside my comfort zone, do hard things, confront situations that I'd rather run from, deal with conflict wisely, and work on many areas and character flaws in my own life. Not only do they ask me hard questions and help me get back on track when I veer off course but they are also always there to celebrate the successes in my life too. I'm eternally grateful for these three wonderful mentors in my life!

Surround yourself with truth-tellers. In the last few years, I've been heartbroken to watch as multiple high-profile leaders have suffered devastating situations in their lives—from losing their marriages because of affairs to losing their businesses because of mismanagement of funds. As I've dug deeper to learn about their situations,

I've discovered that in almost every case these individuals were surrounded by "yes" men and women—people who idolized these leaders and always said yes to whatever their new ideas or desires were, even if they weren't wise or compromised their moral compass or financial situation. This, in turn, resulted in the leaders having an unhealthy view of themselves, which led, of course, to them carrying out destructive or unwise behavior and practices.

As I've watched these tragic circumstances play out, I've become more convinced of the importance of having truth-tellers in one's life. These are people who have earned the right to speak the truth to you. People you can be completely honest with about how you're feeling and what you're struggling with, whether personal or business-related. In the same vein, these are people who love you for who you are, want you to be the best version of yourself, and will be your biggest cheerleaders when great things happen in your life.

Hire a coach. If you can afford it, hire someone short-term to help coach you in areas that you're currently seeking to improve. I hired a proposal writer and ghost editor for my previous book as well as this one. She has made a world of difference in the writing journey—helping me think, process, plan, and write in a more organized and efficient manner. I also have worked with a speaking coach on multiple presentations. Among many other things, she has helped train me in how to wisely approach the art and craft of speaking and shaved hours of prep time off my plate too.

Attend conferences, workshops, and other events. The contacts and relationships I've made at conferences and other personal- and business-development events have been invaluable in helping shape me as a blogger and business owner. If you have the opportunity to attend a writing, speaking, marketing, blogging, social media, or business conference—go! And go with gusto! Use every minute to network and learn. Ask questions of everyone you meet. Talk to keynote speakers and pick their brains. Take notes. Develop action plans and then come home and put them in place!

Growing as an individual will present you with opportunities you would have never had otherwise. I love the e-mail I received from Jenny. When she was laid off from her job a year ago, she viewed the life change as an open door to learn more about herself and pursue her passion. A year after losing her job, she graduated from a health coaching course and is in the process of setting up her own business. She also started her own blog. She writes, "I feel successful right now—even without my first paying client—because I know I am in the right field. I have grown so much this year, and it feels so good!"

Focus on the Progress You Are Making

If you're discouraged that your business isn't growing as fast as someone else's, remember to compare yourself with yourself only. Refocus your energy on the progress you are making. There will always be another business owner doing a better job in some area or another. Don't let it discourage you. Look at the progress you are making toward your goals—even if it seems very slow and miniscule—and be encouraged by that.

While having standards in place to measure your profit and growth margins is important, you must also set your sight on the lessons you are learning and the character you are developing—not on how you're coming up short from where you want to be. You aren't going to make a home run every time, but if you learn and grow while you're at the plate swinging, you're headed in the right direction.

Don't give up! Persistence always pays off, just not always in the way that we expect. Sometimes the unexpected benefits of hard work and persistence are so much better than even our biggest dreams and ambitions.

Your Rent Is Due

As I packed for a recent trip, I was listening to my new podcast "addiction," *EntreLeadership*. (Now I know why my husband has been telling me over and over that I must start listening to it!)

Chris LoCurto was interviewing Rory Vaden, *New York Times* best-selling author of *Take the Stairs*, on the topic of procrastination. Truthfully, I'm not sure what all they said about it because I got stuck on this one phrase Vaden said:

Success is not owned; it's rented—and the rent is due every day.[4]

What a powerful statement. Stop and ponder that for a minute.

Many often think that once we reach a certain level of success— like when we finally bring home a six-figure salary, when we have enough employees where we can sit back and they do all the work for us, when *Entrepreneur* magazine calls to run a story about our successful business—we'll have "made it." But truly, there is never a point in which someone, or even a business, has truly "arrived."

Think about what happens when a CEO of a multi-million-dollar company stops paying rent. When he or she checks out, starts making foolish decisions, or starts spending money without accounting for it, the company, no matter how successful, is eventually going to topple. We've seen this happen many times in the last decade. If a talented basketball player stops working out, eats whatever he wants, and doesn't show up for practice, his career is going to be over very quickly.

If a highly-acclaimed blogger with a large audience stops blogging, doesn't respond to e-mails, never posts on Facebook, and just disappears from the face of the earth for a while, people are going to eventually stop visiting the blog.

If you want to be successful at anything in life, you have to be willing to pay the rent. If you want your business to grow and continue growing and being profitable financially or otherwise, you have to work hard, persevere, and keep at it even when you would rather be doing something else.

Complacency is a killer. Being stagnant—when it comes to personal or business growth—will dampen the progress you've made and keep you from building bigger and better.

Bridget faced this very problem. A homeschooling mom, she taught voice and violin lessons. In the beginning of her venture, she was careful not to overextend herself and only accepted a certain number of students to maintain a flexible schedule. This is good! It's wise to keep realistic expectations and cultivate a healthy work-life balance.

However, as the years passed, she became so comfortable with her long-term students that she stopped advertising, relying only on word-of-mouth. Recently, she was faced with a very diminished studio when half of her students headed off to college. She writes,

I've had to start all over again, getting the word out. In the meantime, my family has had to tighten their belts, a problem I could have avoided if I had stayed on the ball with my advertising!

Find a balance between a healthy personal life and healthy business growth. More importantly, don't get so comfortable that you stop growing and come face-to-face with an unexpected reality. Continue to evaluate your business as it grows or as time passes. Seasons change. Financial situations change. Responsibilities change. Make sure whatever your life situation, you continue to pay your rent. And remember . . .

- Customers aren't going to come banging on your door begging for product unless you reach out to them.
- Your inbox isn't going to be full of e-mails requesting your services unless you make yourself known in the market.
- Your business probably isn't going to expand if you sleep in, don't follow up with people, drop the ball, and don't follow through with commitments you've made.

Every day you have an opportunity to pay the rent toward your current or future success. You can choose to make little steps in the right direction—going to that networking event instead of shopping for another pair of shoes, blogging instead of watching mindless reality TV, learning new marketing ideas instead of aimlessly scrolling through your Facebook feed, taking classes instead of complaining.

The choice is yours. What are you doing today to pay the rent on your future success?

What Gets in the Way

Never be afraid to try something new. Remember,
amateurs built the ark; professionals built the Titanic.

—UNKNOWN

I'M GRATEFUL THAT PINTEREST WASN'T INVENTED BEFORE
I started blogging. If it had been, I doubt I would have ever followed
through with the idea to start a blog; I would have been too intimidated by all the other much more amazing and experienced bloggers
out there and would have felt inadequate.

I still have moments when I feel insecure. Just a few weeks ago,
I was being interviewed for a podcast show and the host asked me,
"So, Crystal, did you ever have moments in the beginning when you
wanted to quit?" I chuckled and then responded something like, "Um,
I still have plenty of moments like that!"

In fact, this very week, I told my husband, "I feel like quitting."
Yes, I really said those exact words.

I don't share this with you to scare you, but to let you know that feeling overwhelmed, wanting to throw in the towel, and getting frustrated when it seems hard work isn't paying off are all parts of the process. And they don't necessarily all go away once you reach a certain level of success.

You bought this book because you want to make a difference in your finances. Maybe you want to get out of debt. Maybe you want to pay off your college loans. Maybe you're saving for a vacation. Maybe you need the money just to survive, to pay the basics like food and rent.

By now, you've read enough stories of women who were able to successfully reach their goals that you're inspired and motivated to pursue possibilities.

But even if you're optimistic of one day reaching your definition of financial freedom, there may be a part of you that is hesitant.

Unsure.

Afraid.

Insecure.

You may carry some doubts that you have what it takes. These fears may hold you back from plunging into or continuing to execute your goals and follow through with the action steps you've outlined.

I'm going to talk about some of those saboteurs in this chapter. If you feel as though you don't have enough time to make the money you need, or if you wonder how you can pull off a commitment to a job or business while balancing your needs and those of your family, this chapter is for you. We'll also cover those feelings of insecurity that might be creeping up and those voices in your head that are telling you your plan is going to fail and you should just give up now.

Manage Your Time, Your Life, and Your Work

Jennifer works three days a week outside of her home. On her days "off," she is busy building three other part-time businesses. This is not easy to do. The hours are demanding and limit the time she can spend with her family. Jennifer feels more and more burned out each passing day. While earning extra income is important, she is slowly starting to realize that it's not more important than being a healthy (and sane) mom and wife. If she doesn't commit to balancing her dreams with her home life, something is bound to break—like her sanity. And when that happens, no one is happy.

Whether you plan on earning extra money through nannying, opening a local consignment shop, bookkeeping for companies, or selling handmade blankets on eBay, you need to figure out how much time you can realistically devote to your entrepreneurial endeavors. This, of course, is going to vary depending on your situation.

If you are a single mom and sole provider, you may have no choice but to make this a full-time gig. If you have older kids in school most of the day, you may have more than a few hours here and there. If your little ones aren't in school and are home with you, you may be more limited in your time. Work with what you have. Find time when you can. I'll give you some pointers on time management in a bit, but I want to first address the importance of a healthy work-life-home balance.

When I first started experimenting with blogging, I was also forging relationships with other online businesses, one of which happened to be with a family who published a nationwide homeschooling magazine. They mentioned they were looking for someone to join their team on a part-time basis helping with marketing responsibilities. I inquired further and discovered the opening entailed researching and contacting companies to build cross-promotion opportunities. I was pretty sure this was something I could handle, and it only required about two hours a day, so I applied and was accepted for the position.

The work was tedious, and often resulted in dead ends, but in the process I learned so much about creating pitches and marketing a product. Best of all, I was getting paid for my time!

After a few months of working in this part-time capacity, this company offered me a more permanent position heading up some of their promotions and helping to brainstorm creative marketing ideas. I was honored and excited about the opportunity, but I didn't stop to think how it would affect my already-full schedule.

At the time, my husband was in law school and working part-time. Also, because we were a one-car family and living in a town where we knew very few people, most days, I was home all day long with our baby girl, Kathrynne. Our family needed the money, and the job helped pass the time at home. Plus, I loved the challenge of it!

I worked hard and gave it my all. The company rewarded me by promoting me to the position of marketing manager and offered a side position of managing an ad sales team. I accepted both opportunities without a lot of thought. I loved what I was doing, the money was a huge blessing, and it gave me something to pour my time and energy into while Jesse was in law school and working. Looking back, I should have thought long and hard before adding more to my plate—especially since I was already stretched too thin running my own growing online business while caring for a baby.

I threw myself wholeheartedly into these new positions. I committed to reading informative books on marketing. I observed other companies and analyzed what worked for them. In addition, I started experimenting with different approaches to find what would be highly successful for this company.

It was rewarding to see my hard work pay off. Magazine sales increased, my team generated a number of ad sales, and I helped to spearhead multiple marketing initiatives. I loved just about every minute of my job. There was only one problem: with my enormous responsibilities for the magazine and my own blog and online business, I found myself working all the time.

Exhaustion quickly set in. I worked well into most nights, praying my daughter would sleep through and save me from being interrupted. I even had to pull occasional all-nighters. The excessive hours I spent working definitely took a toll on me. I look back at photos of me during that time, and I can't believe how sleep-deprived and stressed out I looked. I was so tired it was hard to even fake a smile.

The good news was that between the various work I was doing from home and my husband's part-time income, I was able to stay home with our daughter. Not only were we able to stay out of debt, but for the very first time since being married, our family finally had a little breathing room in our budget. These were good things! Still, there was no way I could continue the unrealistic pace without breaking.

When my husband finished his last week of law school, we felt it was time for me to quit working for the magazine and focus on our home, our family, and my business. I learned so much from this time and am grateful for the experience. While a definite bonus was getting what felt like a college degree in marketing, I also learned my limits. I discovered working sixty to seventy hours a week was not something that belonged in my bucket list, no matter how good the pay!

Now, I still have a number of days when my work-life-family balance is somewhat out of whack. I sometimes spend too much time working and not enough time just enjoying life. I don't always give my family the full attention they deserve because I'm finishing up a project that ended up taking a few hours longer than I expected. My laundry pile is usually larger than I'd like. But while I have my moments and days, I'm encouraged to see how far I've come. Today more than ever, I feel so much healthier. I'm able to devote more time to my kids. And I'm more invested in my marriage and outside friendships than I ever have been before.

A business can take over your life if you don't set boundaries. You need to consider how much time you have to invest in your business or idea. Two to three hours a day? Ten, twenty, or forty hours a week? How much time can you commit to working without getting the life sucked out of your energy, your relationships, and your general well-being?

I talked about Beth in the last chapter. One struggle for her as a single mom who homeschools her children is finding dedicated work time. She says,

> My kids are always home with me, so I am constantly interrupted while I'm working. Maybe it is harder as a single mom because there's no one else to listen to the kids or spend time with them. I feel guilty when I have to tell my daughter to leave me alone so I can work. She doesn't always understand, because I'm sitting right there in the living room so I should be available to talk or look at her latest doodle. There are times when I have to spend more hours on my business than usual (like the holiday selling season). My income is what supports our family so

I have no choice but to work. I am so blessed to be able to do it from home and still homeschool my kids, but in some ways that can be harder because there's no separation between work and family/home life.

Finding a balance between work and life, especially when you're running a business from home, is a challenge, one that often needs to be re-evaluated, tweaked, and given a fresh perspective. Work with whatever works at the time and recognize that change is constant. Above all else, hold dear to your heart what matters most.

While I love my community on Facebook, have met incredible people on Twitter, and love connecting with people on Instagram, I am not a rule follower. I don't want to be chained to a blogging and social media schedule, even though that's what many "experts" say is what will continue to bring in business. If I spend most of my time trying to crank out posts and feed the social media beast, I have no life. Just a blog that rules my life. I want my blog to be a blessing to my family, not a burden, an outpouring of my life, not my whole life.

As much as you can, seek to find a healthy balance between investing in the work necessary to inch your way to financial freedom and maintaining a healthy personal life. Be wise. Know how much time you can spend, set boundaries for that time, and do your best to prioritize and manage that time well.

Time Management Tips

In my book *Say Goodbye to Survival Mode*, I talked in great detail about time management. While I won't repeat the information, I'll offer you some valuable tips on how to let time serve you, not the other way around.

When you start a home business, open a local store, or create a product line to sell online, a common challenge is finding a healthy balance between working and taking care of your family and daily responsibilities. I'm going to assume, like me, you want to avoid burnout from working the dreaded sixty- to seventy-hour week. The following principles will help guide your approach to making the most of your time.

Set parameters for your time. Based on the number of hours you commit to working each day, break them down into chunks. For example, a few months ago, my daily computer time was broken down into the following specific blocks:

- forty-five minutes on substantive writing
- one and a half hours posting time-sensitive deals
- thirty minutes on e-mail
- fifteen minutes on Facebook and Twitter
- fifteen minutes on a writing project
- forty-five minutes extra—placing online orders, reading blog posts, extra projects

Since seasons change, business needs shift, and the market is always evolving, I do my best to be flexible. This means that I can't have a daily schedule like the above set in stone. It's just a loose guide for a season. As change presents itself, I adapt my schedule and time parameters with it.

For instance, I'm currently putting a lot of effort into growing my Facebook interaction and traffic from links posted on Facebook. Because of this, I am spending more time on Facebook-related activities (finding posts to share, scheduling posts for the time when I'm offline, responding to comments on Facebook, and so on) and less time on deal-posting (I've trained one of my team members to help draft some of the deals for me each day to free up time for me to focus on other things). Having a plan, but being flexible and adaptable with that plan, will help you to be much more successful as a business owner.

Also, if you work from home, keep set hours. When you're scheduled to work, work. Don't answer the doorbell unless it's an emergency. Direct all non-business-related calls to voice mail. And don't mindlessly browse the web, decide your baseboards need a deep cleaning, or read and respond to every single e-mail that comes in (especially if it's not urgent or important). Focus on your most important work priorities during your work hours.

Get a grip on social media. Twitter, Facebook, and Skype have made it possible for us to have discussions and online interactions with dozens and even hundreds and thousands of people every day. If used wisely, social media can be a tool to grow your blog or business and reach a wider audience. On the flip side, social media can suck up a great deal of time if not kept in check.

I've definitely struggled with this. As a work-at-home, home-schooling mom of young children, I found that the lure of social media was great. And I wasn't disciplined enough to shut it off. I constantly felt the need to check in on Skype to see what discussions were going on, or to check Twitter to see what I was missing out on, or scroll through endless Facebook feeds to see what other bloggers and friends were up to.

Use social media to help catapult your business and invest in free advertising opportunities, but don't let it rule your life.

Say no often. As women, we're often afraid to say no. We fear we might miss out on some grand opportunity, and we worry about what other people might think of us. I know, because I'm in that position a lot.

I encourage you (and myself!) to guiltlessly say no. If an opportunity is going to require time you don't have or going to oblige you in a way you don't feel comfortable with or is not a good fit for you, your family, your business, or your blog, say no. And focus on the best things that deserve your yes.

The Fear of Failure

I love what John Wooden, renowned and beloved basketball player and coach, said, "Failure is not fatal, but failure to change might be."[1] I found that what keeps many of us from trying something new or different, even if it has the potential to change our lives, is the fear of failure.

We start out hopeful, enthusiastic. But as time passes, the rushing waters of excitement trickle into faint drops of fear or disappointment. Perhaps you weren't able to land that big client. Perhaps the launch of your website or blog wasn't as groundbreaking as you expected. Perhaps you found a flaw in the product you spent years creating and tweaking. Perhaps you find yourself working harder than ever without a profit that makes it worth it.

We fail. Sometimes in small portions, sometimes so paramount we are tempted to close the doors on our business or idea for good. While failure to some degree is inevitable, the important question becomes, "Then what?"

Shelli admitted that when she got married, she and her husband weren't wise financial stewards. Neither one of them learned how to manage money well, so it wasn't long before they found themselves buried under a mountain of debt. When they had their first child, gaining control of their finances became a priority. While Shelli desired to be a stay-at-home mom, she also wanted to contribute to remedying their debts. Having written for her high school and college newspapers and local magazines, she figured she could write and earn some extra money in her spare time. Eleven years have passed since that time, and Shelli hasn't made much money writing.

She writes,

It seems so hard to find legitimate writing opportunities. There are a lot of websites that offer jobs, but many seemed to send me on a wild goose chase or pay only a few dollars for hours of work. I've written dozens of articles and pitches that I haven't gotten paid for. I have a blog that I have not made a dime off of. I am overwhelmed with information about writing. I've read books about writing and blogging, but feel like it is hard to put so much time and effort into a process that may not make any money. It also seems like there are so many great writers out there that the market is flooded.

Shelli is so exasperated that she wonders if she should give up her dream or keep trying. I know Shelli is not alone. There might come a day when the effort you expend to bring extra money to your household does not pay off. So . . . what do you do?

Before you decide to quit your business, below are some ideas to think about:

- *Take a sabbatical.* Sometimes we think we need to quit when really we're just tired. When bloggers come to me to tell me they are shutting down their site, I encourage them to instead take a two-to four-week break. Time away from your business will usually give you clarity that you can't have when you're so busy just trying to make it through each day.
- *Revisit and evaluate your business action plan and processes.* Tweak, revise, and rethink some of your steps. Maybe bad processes or poor planning is what is bogging you down.
- *Determine if there is one particular problem that's shadowing your success.* Could it be lack of time? High expenses? Poor customer base? Get advice from experts, read books on the topic, and research solutions.
- *Talk to close friends and colleagues you trust and respect.* Get their counsel. They may have the right perspective you need.

If you do all of these things and you still feel like quitting is the right thing, then quit. Remember, not every business is going to hit a home run. As was the case with my wedding business, some ideas are just gigantic learning opportunities or stepping-stones for better things to come. If you do shut down your business, don't let that experience define you as a failure. Instead, use it to shape and help you continue to grow.

Sometimes failure can be a conduit for finding what works. When Jamie and her husband had been married for a year, they determined to get their finances on track. After brainstorming ideas to bring home extra income, she remembered a family member who had a portrait photography business that raked in thousands of dollars per session. Since her husband loved photography, landscape in particular, she pushed him to consider portrait photography. Though reluctant at first, he agreed.

It was a disaster. While he was a talented photographer, the economy wasn't that great and the market couldn't support the prices he needed to charge in order to turn a profit. Also, editing the photographs turned out to be more of a hassle than they considered. They would spend forty to eighty hours a week retouching pictures only to have the client purchase nothing.

While the business tanked, here's the good news: Jamie's husband realized his true love and his passion—nature photography—and began to pursue that instead. He got his passion for his hobby back. And Jamie, ever the entrepreneur, took the steps to begin the writing and speaking business that she had dreamed of for years. Now in its fourth year, Jamie's business is thriving. She and her husband are both living their dreams!

I commend this couple for actually doing something, for stepping out into the unknown in order to begin creating financial breathing room. Sure, the initial idea may not have worked out in their favor, but it paved the way for them to create an idea that finally worked!

Failure can be a conduit for finding your niche. Dekota has found this to be true. She writes,

I tried virtual assisting back when my daughter was teeny tiny and, from my experience at the time, it is a very difficult field to get into. Unless you have a specific skill, offering basic clerical services will hardly land a client! After many tries at jobs like medical transcriptionist, bookkeeping, among MANY other things, I found my calling. I make jewelry now, which I love, and it has brought in enough income so my husband was able to quit his job and become a stay-at-home dad.

Just Plain Ole Fear

Thinking about the possibility of failure is just one of many fears that plague us, that keep us stuck, that keep us from reaching or even trying to reach our goals.

I know the power of being afraid. All my life, I have battled fear. I've worried what people would think. I have thought in worst-case scenarios. I've feared the unknown, the known, and the might-happen. In the process, I have wasted a lot of time and energy on fear.

In the last few years, I've been blessed to meet people who are challenging me to stop living in fear and start living in faith. Fear paralyzes. Faith frees. Punching fear in the face has been a very stretching experience. It's not been a onetime thing, either (oh, how I wish it were that easy!). I've had to get up and go face the fear monsters over and over again.

But each and every time that I step outside my comfort zone and confront my fears, there have been rich rewards. And it has been every bit worth it.

Does jumping out of the safe zone scare you? Well, then take a tiny baby step. And then another tiny baby step. Whatever you do, though, don't stay put.

One thing that helps me is to ask myself, "What's the worst thing that can happen?" If you ask yourself this question, in most cases there are only two "worst-case scenario" outcomes: (1) you fail—which isn't necessarily a terrible thing, as we talked about earlier; or

(2) you decide you don't like it. In that case, there are a million other possibilities you can try next.

I love this quote from Michael Hyatt: "The really important stuff happens just outside your comfort zone." [2] I've found this to be true in my own life. There are so many amazing experiences, relationships, and opportunities I would have missed out on if I had stayed in the safe zone.

Sure, it's frightening, but if you're willing to take the risk, I can almost guarantee that you'll end up finding it really rewarding. Plus, I've discovered that when you start pushing yourself outside your comfort zone, your comfort zone moves. Things that were once completely daunting to you can become exhilarating and invigorating. And no matter what happens when you get outside of your comfort zone, it will be more inspiring than staying stuck in a rut.

When Others Stand in Your Way

Whether you are considering working with a direct-marketing company selling cosmetics, starting your own commercial cleaning service, or providing consultant work to local businesses, you might come face-to-face with people, even those closest to you, who shed some doubt your way. They may say things like:

"Why don't you just get a regular job?"
"I know someone who tried that and it didn't work."
"Is that the best idea you could come up with?"

Now, for the purpose of this section, I'm not talking about the people in your life who can offer legitimate advice grounded in wisdom and experience. You should certainly consider and receive knowledge from people who have something valuable to say. However, if your business idea or plan is being picked apart by Negative Nelly and there's no basis for the negativity, you must stop letting her bring you down. You can't control what other people say about you, but you can control how you let it affect you.

There will always be people who disagree with you, criticize the choices you've made in life, or are just plain negative. That's a fact of life. The surest way to live a miserable life is to try to please everyone. It's impossible . . . but you can sure run yourself ragged trying.

Don't allow the negative opinions of others to scatter fear in your path. Tactfully remove yourself from negative people and situations as much as you can. When it's not possible to avoid the negativity, picture an invisible shield between you and the negative people and tune out their unfounded attacks.

In addition, do not respond to negativity with more negativity. That only fuels the fire. Either don't respond at all or respond with genuine love and kindness.

What Do You Have to Offer? (A Lot!)

My husband and I attended a conference last year with some incredibly talented thinkers and doers. The combined experiences and backgrounds of the speakers and attendees provided much collective wisdom. Almost the entire conference, I felt like my mind was going to explode with all of the new information I was gleaning.

But you know one of the things that stuck out for me most about the entire experience? It wasn't the knowledge, the noteworthy résumés, or the impressive achievements. It was that many of these amazingly talented people struggle with insecurity.

In fact, two of the people I would consider to be some of the most accomplished individuals at the conference both confided in me that they felt out of place.

And I totally got it, because I felt the exact same way. At each meal or roundtable discussion, I would meet people who had done so much with their lives—and I would want to sink smaller and smaller into my chair.

At one point in the Q&A discussion, I'm not sure what possessed me, but I raised my hand to share something. As soon as they gave me the microphone, I literally froze with fear. In that split second, terror registered in my brain: *Why on earth did I raise my hand? Do I really think I had anything worthwhile to add to the discussion?* Oh how I wished right then and there that the ground would just swallow me whole.

I somehow managed to say something semi-coherent, handed back the mic, sat down, and felt like a colossal failure. More thoughts flooded through my head: *Why am I at a conference on launching a speaking business when I can't even stand up and say four sentences without failing? Why am I saying "yes" to these speaking opportunities when there are millions of people out there who could do the job a thousand times better than I could?*

Still, a part of me knew I didn't have to resort to drowning in insecurities. Oh sure, I had plenty of inadequacies and shortcomings I could mull over, but focusing on them would do me no good. I had to set aside those emotional chains and focus on positive truths, such as *I am enough. And I have a purpose.*

You know what? You, too, are enough. And you, too, have a purpose.

You may know someone or a handful of people who have started their business and met tremendous success in a short time. Or whose blog took off immediately after the first post. Or whose business idea made them hundreds of thousands of dollars in the first two years.

If that's not your story, it's because you have your own. And it's enough. Your worth is not established in how successful or smart you are or how much debt you're able to pay off in two months or how quickly you can grow your blog or business. You have a unique perspective, experience, and insight that can bless and impact others in a way that someone else with a different story might not be able to.

Yes, it's important and I highly encourage you to keep challenging yourself to grow, strengthen your weak zones, and learn and apply as much as you can. But you're not going to be perfect and have the perfect business idea with the perfect action plan and the perfect way of doing things to bring home the perfect amount of money to make a difference.

The rest of the chapters of this book are devoted to intertwining purpose with making money. Yes, it's possible. And it's about perspective. But before you dig in and start reading, take a break. Pause. Breathe. Allow the following words to sink in.

I am enough. I was created for a purpose.

Aside from believing in the possibilities and opportunities that await you and your loved ones in changing your financial direction for the better, I want you to own the gifts you were given and truly believe that you were created for a purpose greater than yourself. My hope is for you to fully experience how great an impact you can make, even while you establish your financial future.

8

Live Generously

I am only one, but I am one. I cannot do everything,
but I can do something. And I will not let what
I cannot do interfere with what I can do.

—EDWARD EVERETT HALE

THREE YEARS AGO, MISTY'S GRANDMOTHER SUFFERED A
stroke that triggered the early onset of dementia. Though newly married, Misty and her husband welcomed the elderly woman, who had raised her as a child, to come live with them. This gracious granddaughter transitioned out of her full-time job as a paralegal into a work-at-home position for her firm at fewer hours and a decrease in salary. Still, Misty was able to be home and care for her ailing grandmother, as well as pay for some necessary medical treatment.

The financial responsibility, however, quickly became a hardship. The bills piled up so fast, Misty couldn't afford to pay them in light of her pay cut. So she started thinking of clever ways to supplement her income. First, she started selling Scentsy products and used the profit earned as start-up capital to obtain her art dealer's license. This propelled her to start selling her arts and crafts locally, which spurred on an additional Etsy crafting business.

In under two years, Misty used the money she made selling her art locally to pay off her grandmother's outstanding medical bills of $16,000. Through her three business ventures as well as a savings blog she started, she also made enough money to pay off her personal debt, undergraduate student loans, expenses not covered by grants for her and her husband to go back to school, and to fund her other passion, sponsoring small business loans through KIVA.org for other women, mothers, and community leaders. Misty writes,

> These small homespun ventures have helped me to have the breathing room and financial freedom I longed for. Though I have leaps and bounds to go, I feel blessed to no longer worry about vet bills, grooming expenses, school fees, unexpected child, car, and home repair costs, co-pays for my family, or paying for health insurance for myself. Three years ago I started with $100.00 and have snowballed these funds into three businesses and a better way of life for my family.

Amazing, right? Now, though these accomplishments are certainly admirable, I love that Misty says her biggest triumph was being able to pay cash for her grandmother to reside in a long-term care facility that could provide her with the full-time medical attention she needed considering her worsening illness. Misty's grandmother is now living debt-free in a beautiful, safe, and nurturing environment.

Purposeful Earning

Misty took initiative to help impact the future of someone who had made a difference in her own life. She is one of hundreds of women I know who have found creative ways to earn income for a purpose. Read those last three words again.

For. A. Purpose.

- not to fatten a bank account
- not to buy the latest gadgets
- not to say we have
- not so others can admire a fancy car in our driveway
- not so we can win an award for Best Website of the Year
- not so we can wow others with our innovative marketing plans

We should focus on making money to impact our family and loved ones for the better. In addition, our focus for making money should be to help those who are struggling in our community and around the world. In this book, you've read many stories of women who have reclaimed financial freedom by earning income to pay off debt, support their families single-handedly, invest in schooling, and support causes they are passionate about and believe in. These women have tapped into the core of financial freedom and developed the appetite to live generously.

We live in a world steeped in consumerism. Author Clive Hamilton wrote, "In the marketing society, we seek fulfillment but settle for abundance. Prisoners of plenty, we have the freedom to consume instead of the freedom to find our place in the world."[1] The misguided messages that crawl into our brains, from advertisements, TV shows, magazines, even friends and strangers, determine our value, our focus, and our priorities. We are almost trained to feel happiest when we have more. We find meaning in bigger and better. We spend and spend and spend some more to look and feel good.

But we weren't created to be consumers. We were made for more. We are destined to be stewards, wise managers of not just our money but also our time, our values, and our priorities.

I recognize that some of you reading this book are in dire financial straits. Earning income is a matter of survival. I get that, and I'm not here to make you feel bad or un-generous because your stomach is in knots trying to figure out how to scrounge up money to keep the lights on next month.

During the first few years of our marriage, when things were tighter than tight, we couldn't afford to give generously to causes we believed in because every penny of our income was needed to keep a roof over our heads and food on the table. There wasn't room to do more than keep our commitment to a weekly tithe to our local church. Oh, we often donated our time and energy to help others or gave away extra items (like toiletries and household products) that I had gotten for free by pairing coupons with sales. We also tried to live as frugally as possible with the hope that someday soon we would be in a better financial position to give.

So if you're in a season where you're just scraping by, don't be discouraged. In the next chapter, I'm going to share some ways you can use your business to bless others, even if you don't have a lot of money to spend. In the meantime, I want this chapter to inspire you to think long-term and dream big. If you make wise financial choices—like working hard and sticking with a budget—eventually, you'll likely be in a place where it doesn't just make a difference in your household budget, it will also allow you to make a big difference in the lives of others.

Finding the Right Heart Space

Managing our money well can be a challenge. It requires sacrifice, selflessness, and stewardship. It means constantly taking inventory of our hearts, our desires, our longings.

As a writer on frugality and money-saving tips, I'm frequently asked the same types of questions about how to save, when you should spend, and what you should spend your money on. When I'm being interviewed for various media pieces, more often than not, I find that the interviewer sticks with practical questions, like asking for tips on how to cut a grocery bill.

While I'm more than happy to offer suggestions (hey, it's one of the ways I make my living), I always try to steer the conversation away from the "how-to" and toward the "why."

You see, all of the money-saving tricks in the world are going to be meaningless if you're not in the right heart space when it comes to finances—for example, if you view money as a path to happiness, or are constantly worried about not having enough, or think that winning the lottery is the ticket to finding ultimate peace, or see money as a tool to get bigger and better.

I like what the writer Samuel Johnson wrote: "People need to be reminded more often than they need to be instructed."[2] That being said, this section is not a lesson in frugal living; it is, however, a spotlight on intention. Consider why you want to earn more money.

If it's just so you can buy more stuff, I can tell you right now that it's not worth it. The more you have, the more you'll want. It will never be enough.

If you want to live an amazingly fulfilling life, you must live for something bigger than yourself, something besides material desires, words of praise from others, or a long list of accolades. Start focusing on making a difference. Think long and hard about what matters most.

Last summer, Colorado suffered an epidemic of wildfires. Many people we knew or knew of lived close to these deadly fires and had to evacuate their communities multiple times not knowing if when they returned their houses would still be standing. While none of our friends experienced any damage, sadly, a friend of a friend ended up losing her home as a result of a wildfire that engulfed her neighborhood.

This particular family was heading out the door to attend a soccer game when they were ordered by local officials to evacuate their home. This was just one out of many evacuations within the last few days, so they didn't give it much thought and in a rush to make the soccer game on time, grabbed only a few personal items from their home. Shockingly, a few days passed before they were allowed to return to their neighborhood, during which time they received no word as to the extent of damage to their property. When the phone call finally came, it was devastating news: their entire home and all of their belongings had burned to the ground.

I spent a day with the mother of this family a few weeks after the tragedy. As she recounted the story to me, tears filled her eyes. She told me how traumatic it was to return to the charred rubble and sift through what was left of her possessions, nothing but a deep pile of ashes.

Over the next few weeks, I couldn't stop replaying our conversation. I kept imagining what it would be like to, in the blink of an eye, lose everything I owned except for the clothes on my back. I kept contemplating: is my fulfillment found in what I own? Or in the possessions I have? Or in the money that's in the bank?

While this family didn't lose the money in the bank and they eventually received a settlement from their insurance company to replace most of the items that had been destroyed, save for sentimental things like pictures, their story served as a great reminder to me—my fulfillment has to be in something more than the stuff I own and the money I make, because, really, all of that could be taken away at any moment without any warning.

A Wider Lens

Here's the deal, folks. Money itself doesn't satisfy. There's got to be a bigger purpose than just to make it and have it and then make more and have more. In her book *Love, Skip, Jump: Start Living the Adventure of Yes*, author Shelene Bryan wrote, "I'm not concerned that you'll fail at something. I'm concerned that you'll succeed at something that doesn't matter."[3]

There are many, many things we can devote our time and effort to. There are a multitude of ways to succeed in life. But there are only a few things that truly matter in the long run.

In chapter 4 I mentioned Nicole Johnson, founder of the Baby Sleep Site. In one of our e-mail exchanges, she included details about the success of her business.

Her website welcomes over five hundred thousand visitors per month. She anticipates being a $1-million-in-revenue company within the next two to three years. All ten of her employees work from home, including Nicole, providing a healthy life balance. These are all wonderful things, and while I certainly applaud her, what really struck me about the e-mail was what Nicole said meant most to her.

> The very best part is that we are helping other families and it is so rewarding! We get emails from people all the time about how we've changed their lives, saved their marriages, and made happier families.

This, folks, is what it's all about. Life is ultimately not about the traffic numbers, the amazing marketing techniques, or the income generated. It's about impact—the impact you make on the lives of others.

Over the course of the last ten years, I've received my fair share of criticism for what I do. I get it all—from random, rude drive-by comments, strange e-mails from people over-sharing weird pet peeves, and the just plain crazy and negative commentaries. Some people even send long e-mails detailing their deep concerns over how I've chosen to live my life. Much as I want to, I've challenged myself to not immediately hit the delete key as soon as I read the first few words of what I know will be a negative editorial. I take the time to read the critique and then search my heart to see if there is any truth to what the person says. Many times, I find an area or heart attitude in my life that needs some re-evaluation or development. But other times, these perceptions are nothing more than a nay-saying rant, and I realize that I just have to be okay with disappointing certain readers. After all, they don't know my husband, me, or my kids personally, nor the details of our situation.

Probably one of the most bothersome kinds of e-mails and comments that come my way are from people who are upset by the fact that I make money from my blog. Even a few friends and acquaintances have voiced their disapproval over my income-earning strategies from not only blogging but also my writing and speaking opportunities.

Just last week, I was hanging out with a friend I love dearly. In the course of our conversation, she looked me in the eye and said, "Crystal, you believe you should make more money so you can give more, right?" Before I had the chance to respond, she continued without missing a beat. "Because I disagree with you on that."

I was struck by her rather bold comment, but I realized she had a false understanding of what I believe. I had to pause for a moment to think how to explain to her that my goal isn't to make more money, but rather to make an impact while also having a healthy balance in my life. After a minute, I responded, "My goal is about being a good steward of what I have, using my platform, energy, time, talent, even money to make a difference." My friend was surprised by my remarks. And the conversation reminded me that I need to make sure the message I'm living lines up with my ultimate goal—impacting others for the better.

In chapter six I talked about Beth, a single mom who provided for her family by selling items on Amazon. While she is excited that her tremendous business growth has been able to sustain her family through hard times, she wants to do more. There are dreams birthed inside of her, ways she believes she can give back to others. Beth writes, "I'm still believing for even greater provision so I can focus on the real desire of my heart—ministering to other moms, especially single ones."

When Beth was on staff at a local church some odd years ago, she noticed that many moms were struggling, whether dealing with depression, feeling crushed by the weight of responsibilities and demands, or being emptied of energy and passion. Some of them needed nothing more than a word or two of encouragement; others needed greater support. Beth loved being able to have deep conversations with these women, sharing with them her own story of leaving behind a toxic relationship and raising her children.

Years later, Beth has never lost the desire to reach out to fellow mothers and is trying to figure out what that will look like in a more permanent way, perhaps writing a book or starting a single mother's ministry in her area. Even as she is researching her options, Beth continues to passionately share and encourage any mom she meets. She gets it! I love that Beth is focused on nurturing the desire in her heart to help other moms.

While Beth aligns her priorities with what matters, other entrepreneurs do not. In the excitement of starting a business and seeing it take off, it's easy to get so caught up in making it successful that you forget the important goals, the ones that come from the deepest parts of our hearts.

As I shared earlier, I've been guilty of this. I've chased after numbers, dollar signs, and accolades. And I'm here to tell you it's not worth it. It's exhausting and unfulfilling. And like money, it will never be enough.

While I encourage setting goals and working hard, these things need to be tempered with balance. Yes, I said that elusive word *balance*. We hear it so often, don't we? It seems every day I read an article, blog, or title of a book that tells us how important it is to have balance and how to find it. Here's the thing: I don't think anyone is ever going to achieve a perfect balance. In fact, I believe the very concept of balance is actually the act of continually making small shifts and adjustments in order to not fall off the bandwagon.

I remember watching the live feed of Nik Wallenda as he tightrope walked across the Grand Canyon in the summer of 2013. I held my breath with each step he took and let out a massive sigh of relief when he finally made it to the other side. I was intrigued by him and his story, so I bought and read his book, *Balance: A Story of Faith, Family, and Life on the Line*. I was fascinated by his story and how he became such a successful tightrope walker.

Tightrope walking is an extremely difficult sport. It requires incredible discipline, concentration, and focus. As *Science* magazine says,

> Keeping steady on a stationary plank or beam is hard enough, but a rope adds the destabilizing element of motion. A rope not only sways but also moves in response to a person's movement, forcing the walker to constantly change position.[4]

I think this is also important in our lives. As I've said before, there's never a point when you have arrived. You will constantly need to make small (or sometimes large) tweaks in how you do things, changes in your schedule, and shifts in your priorities.

Evaluate and Shift Your Priorities

In the next chapter I'm going to share more stories of women who have shifted their priorities successfully and also share some ideas for you to begin (or continue on) the purposeful journey of living generously. But for now, I offer a few self-markers to ensure that your heart space continues to lean in the right direction of using what you already have to impact others in a meaningful way rather than chasing after more just because.

Bloom Where You're Planted

The landscape of your business will look different at different times. There will be seasons of plenty, where work abounds and the money follows. And there will likewise be lean times, where demand for your services or products wanes and profits subsequently lessen. Above all, remember to make the most of what you have.

David Sturt is the author of the *New York Times* bestselling book *Great Work: How to Make a Difference People Love.* He has conducted numerous extensive studies over the years and has found a link forging a passion to make a difference with ultimate extraordinary performance, even if your work isn't as glamorous as you'd like. Sturt suggests that anything you do, whether you are a janitor or the CEO of a company, contains the raw materials of greatness. He suggests we run into problems like boredom, frustration, and dissatisfaction when we choose to be distracted by a grandiose vision of potential success only when every external variable is aligned perfectly and set in motion—whether that's dominating a market, having the right team, or making enough money. Alternatively, when we focus on what we have in the present, he says, "our mindset shifts from seeing ourselves as workers with an assignment to crank out to seeing ourselves as people with a difference to make."[5]

Perspective matters. No business is going to be perfect. And not everything is going to go as planned all the time. So in the words of

St. Francis de Sales, "Bloom where you're planted."[6] No matter what your situation, if the money's rolling in or your hard work doesn't seem to be paying off just yet, consider doing the following:

- Keep serving your customers with enthusiasm and gratitude.
- Keep creating top-notch quality products with careful attention to detail.
- Keep working hard to live out the mission statement of your business.
- Keep responding to e-mails, questions, letters, or inquires in a timely manner.
- Keep focusing on the positive things that are happening— however small they seem.
- Keep setting goals, breaking them down into bite-sized pieces, and getting up and working toward them every day.
- Keep taking time to have a healthy balance in life and to make sure you're nurturing your health and relationships.
- Keep believing the best about others—customers and colleagues alike.

Choose Gratitude

When you look around you, there is always someone who seems to have more than you. Or a better business idea. Or a quicker path to success. Or a better product. Or more talents. Or a bigger customer base. Or more money. And on and on it goes.

Life is full of things that don't seem fair. And if you choose to dwell on those things, you can quickly become discouraged, discontent, and downright frustrated. But life is also full of beautiful things—if you look for them. Your perspective and attitude on life won't usually change your circumstances, but they can sure change the way you feel.

Expressing gratitude doesn't require money. It doesn't require much thought or effort. But it can change our whole outlook on life and our business. For instance, just last month, I was approached about an amazing, ongoing national media opportunity. I was blown away by the prospect of being given such a coveted spot and got really pumped up about the possibilities it might open. Part of the process of landing the gig was an interview with the producers and then a trip to New York City for a chemistry test, to see if my personality jived well with the other hosts on this TV show. The producers had sent me a list of questions they wanted to go over on this interview, and with only a few days to prep, I spent hours getting ready, practicing, and even visualizing how well I anticipated it would go. When the day finally came, I was excited beyond words. And then, only a few hours before the interview, I received an e-mail from the producer. "I'm sorry," she wrote. "We're taking a new direction with the show and we're not going to need you at this time."

My heart sank. It was quite the letdown, especially after spending three days psyching myself up. The feeling of disappointment grew into discouragement, simmering in my heart for days. It was time to make a choice between moping and whining that I wasn't chosen or being grateful that I was even considered in the first place. I decided to focus on the latter, and let me tell you, it really changed my perspective. There is always something to be grateful for. If you start looking for things to appreciate, you'll begin to find them all around you.

Last year I developed the habit of keeping a gratitude journal. It helped me to keep a positive, thankful attitude in the midst of some health problems I was experiencing. When I first wake up in the morning, I read my Bible, pray, and write down at least one line of blessings from the past day. Some days are easier than others, but even on a hard day, I can always think up at least a few good things from the day before. Truly, "Gratitude turns what we have into enough."

Be Present, Not Perfect

I loved reading *Bread and Wine: A Love Letter to Life Around the Table with Recipes* by Shauna Niequist. It moved me. It inspired me. It challenged me. And it made me want to spend more time in the kitchen and around the table.

The phrase that stuck out most was this: present over perfect.[7] Shauna shares how we can get so wrapped up in trying to make life perfect—to get all our ducks in a row and keep them that way—that we miss the present.

When you're on a mission to earn extra money, things can get busy quickly. But in the midst of researching, improving, reading, tweaking, expanding, brainstorming, building, creating, and changing, don't forget the life that is happening around you.

It's easy to rush through life with our plans, our goals, and our lists as we check things off. To pat ourselves on the back for being a powerhouse of productivity.

And in the process, we forget to breathe.

To slow down.

To soak up the moments.

To savor the here and now.

No matter where you are in life or what you do, you probably agree that it feels like the work is never done. You can always find more projects to tackle, more e-mails to answer, more phone calls to make, more leads to follow up on, more to research, more to improve, more ways to advertise, more ideas to implement. You have to be your personal boss—whether you are self-employed or not—and choose to put parameters in place. Do what you can do, do the best you can do, and then be okay with that.

Instead of pursuing a life of perfection in my family and in my business, I want to pursue a life of being present. I want to encourage you to do the same.

Here are some ways you can be present:

- Actively listen to the customer who is so appreciative because the health products you sold her truly made a difference.
- Treat a client like a human being instead of a consumer.
- Do something nice for someone who is helping you establish your business.
- Remember to spend time with your loved ones, your family, and your friends even when your inbox is full and you've been up late working.
- Set aside the project with a looming deadline because your child has something exciting he or she wants to tell you or your husband wants to go to the movies with you.
- Go out of your way to celebrate a colleague who has received some exciting news.
- Take time to ask how someone is really doing when you call, instead of just launching into the business question or proposal you called about.
- Set boundaries around your work time so that it doesn't take over your life.

Present, not perfect. That's how I want to live.

Bigger and Better Visions (Not Stuff)

Recently, I finished *The Charge* by Brendon Burchard. While I didn't love that there were curse words in the book, I found some of the parts really inspiring. I especially enjoyed this quote:

> You want to change? Then do not, under any circumstances, allow yourself to settle on a vision or a calling or a simple change in any arena that is uninspiring. If you're going to have clarity on something in your life, make it something so big and bright and shiny that you will get out of bed and chase it until you grasp it or die. Bring forth a desire that knows no safe boundaries and even scares you a little bit, that will demand all the best that is in you, that takes you out of your own orbit and onto new and unfamiliar ground. That kind of desire changes your life, and it changes the world.[8]

Reading these words prompted me to re-evaluate some of my own priorities.

I don't want to look back at the end of my life with regrets that I spent too many hours, days, weeks, and years chasing after something that did little more than pad a bank account.

- I want to make a difference.
- I want to live each day as though it were my last.
- I want to invest my life, my energy, and my time into things that have lasting impact.

Last year, I sat down and typed out some of my greatest life priorities—the things I am committed to wrapping my efforts and time around. Here's what I wrote down:

1. Nurture a vibrant relationship with the Lord. This means that I will take time to read God's Word, pray, read books that encourage and challenge me spiritually, attend a church where I'm being spiritually fed, and surround myself with friends who are pointing me to the Lord and spurring me on to grow closer to the Lord each day.

2. Invest time and effort into my marriage in order that it would be strong, thriving, and last for the long haul. This means that I will show my husband in very practical ways that he is my top priority, that I will expend thought and energy into him, that I will keep the sparks of romance flying, that I will make choices that reflect the priority my husband is to me.

3. Raise children of character who will grow up to be world-changers. This means that I will spend time each week pouring into my kids, that I will listen to them, love them, pray for them, teach them, read to them, give them opportunities to serve alongside me, ask for forgiveness when I react wrongly to them, and do my best to model character before them.

4. Challenge families to get their finances in order so they can be generous givers. This means I will take time to read and research items related to financial issues, that I will write and speak on the subject, that I will continue to learn all I can about financial freedom and money-saving

tactics, that I will listen to the needs my readers are expressing in comments and e-mails and look for ways to provide resources to help meet those needs, and—most importantly—that I will practice what I preach.

5. Inspire women to live with intention and purpose. This means that I will work on living with intention and purpose in my own life, write and speak on this topic, look for new examples and fresh ideas to communicate the ideas of living with intention and purpose to women, and create resources to encourage and inspire women in this.

Will I see all of these things to completion in my lifetime? Only God knows. But I do know that investing my life in impactful ways makes every day worth waking up for. I don't have to wonder whether my life matters. I don't have to wish I could find something to invest my time in to make a difference. I already know what my priorities are; now I just have to get up each day and live them out.

Creating your own plan from this book will make a difference in your finances and your life. I hope you are as excited about this as I am for you. But there's more. Never forget that.

I want you to consider your focus, your priorities, your vision. What are you living for? Are you thinking about long-term goals? Are you just trying to live through the next hour? If you want to live an amazingly fulfilling life, you must live for something bigger than yourself. Stop trying to make yourself happy or comfortable and start focusing on making a difference in someone else's life. You can do this if you are just starting out in your business or even if you're not quite sure what to do yet.

I'm reminded of my good friend Lisa-Jo. An author, world traveler, and a mom of three kids, she believes that "motherhood should come with its own super hero cape."⁹ Lisa-Jo has a heart and vision for women all over the world who spend days changing diapers, shuffling kids around to games and practices, mending scrapes, battling laundry piles—you know, all the mundane yet necessary tasks a mother is charged with, the ones that sometimes make her feel like "just" a mom.

Before Lisa-Jo's book, *Surprised By Motherhood*, was released, I e-mailed her about it and asked how I could help her promote it because it had resonated with me at a deep level. In the course of our e-mail conversation, she told me about the big dream brewing in her heart—she wanted to raise enough money through her blog to improve the village of 150 adults and 250 orphans in Maubane, South Africa. Born and raised in this country and having already been involved with mission work for this particular village, Lisa-Jo's vision was to raise enough money to build a community center, a vegetable garden, some classrooms, a playground, a clean water supply, and more.

Lisa-Jo challenged her blog readers (mostly everyday moms) to "fall in love with the world next door"¹⁰ by offering them opportunities, financial and otherwise, to make a positive impact on the children in this village. Witnessing her passion and heart explode for this project, I was inspired to personally jump on board as well as encourage my readers to participate. The response was amazing. I got goose bumps watching the donations roll in. I received many e-mails from my readers thanking me for letting them know about this opportunity and sharing why they gave and the sacrifices they were happy to make in the process.

Lisa-Jo has ignited a fire in the hearts of hundreds of families across America who have given to date—from a few dollars to a few hundred dollars—a grand total of $50,000 for this village. She was able to do this not because she has hundreds of thousands of blog readers but because she has a fire in her belly and an unrelenting commitment to see change.

Just the other day, I received an e-mail from her with a link to pictures of what that money has translated to in that small South African village. I didn't know whether to cry or shout for joy when I scrolled through the pictures and saw the vegetable garden, the playground, the water supply, and the beginnings of a community center and kitchen.

Lisa-Jo is a great example of how one woman with a vision to do something bigger than herself matters. Through her fearless and compassionate efforts, she has opened the eyes of thousands of women—and not just moms—to discover more meaning, more fulfillment, and a dream beyond the ordinary.

Your passion to impact others may not be raising funds for South Africa, starting a ministry for single moms, helping parents get their babies to sleep through the night, or caring for your elderly grandmother, but there is something stirring in you. Even right now, as you read these words. It doesn't matter how big or how small, whether your reach extends across the globe or across your neighbor's yard. Friend, I say this with every bit of conviction: you were made for more than just surviving the day, making a decent income, living for the weekend, or making your car payment on time.

You were created to make a difference.

How to Give?

Let Me Count the Ways!

I have found that among its other benefits,
giving liberates the soul of the giver.

—MAYA ANGELOU

TWENTY-THREE YEARS AGO, KAREN BECAME AN ENTRE-preneur when she suddenly found herself as a single mom caring for three little ones under the age of four. Believing she should stay at home with her kids but needing a source of income, Karen began making and delivering freshly made sourdough bread and eventually muffins, cookies, and cakes to local businesses and individuals.

The first Christmas in business, a customer asked her to put some of the goodies in a basket. This custom-created product was met with such rave reviews, Karen was inspired to focus her business on creating goodie baskets instead of just baking bread. Thus, the Country Gourmet was born. Karen eventually opened a storefront shop to grow her business and increase her customer base with corporate clients and a local hospital.

Although Karen's priority was being able to provide for her family financially while keeping flexible working hours, she also wanted to make an impact in her community. From the start, she committed 10 percent of her income to the local church and sometimes as much as an additional 20 percent toward widows in need, a local orphanage, a children's home, and missionaries. One Christmas she helped a young couple pay their attorney fees so they could adopt a sweet baby girl.

While some financial advisors have recommended that Karen cut back on her charitable donations to boost her profits, she refuses. She has a heart to give, to make a difference with the opportunity she was given and worked so hard to grow.

I love that! It's inspiring to see someone motivated by others rather than profit margins. This is one way to find meaning and fulfillment in life. It's about recognizing that our world is bigger than our circumstances, our problems, our needs, our desires, and our successes. It's about taking initiative and taking action. It's about finding a need and filling it. Leo Rosten said, "The purpose of life is not to be happy—but to matter, to be productive, to be useful, to have it make some difference that you lived at all."[1]

In 1990, along with the help of a friend, Sarita started Sonlight Curriculum, a small business that provides homeschool curriculum to people, including missionaries. Twenty-five years later, Sonlight is thriving in all fifty states and numerous countries.

Sarita has not only turned an idea she brainstormed in her garage into an international business, she is also intentional in using the business to make an increasingly bigger global difference. Her first project, for instance, empowered over eight thousand women in India to learn to read. Through her business Sarita has been able to increase her own giving (the company gives over 50 percent of profits to charitable organizations). In 2013, they led a team in giving $360,000 toward children's Bible clubs in India.

Establish a Giving Budget

It's great to say that you want to make a difference with your business. And it's fantastic to have a heart to give. But just wanting those things is not enough. Great intentions get you nowhere if you don't back them up with a plan of action.

I encourage you to prioritize purposeful generosity. In the very beginning, right as you set up your business budget, commit some of your earnings toward a "giving budget." This is money that you'll use solely for the purpose of investing in others, donating to a charity, helping someone in need, and so on.

It might be hard to even consider doing this when you first set out in your business venture. After all, those early months may not produce a whole lot of profit. But don't let that discourage you! Establish the practice of giving part of your earnings as soon as you have netted income and it will trickle into an ongoing practice. Not only does living with outstretched arms generate much joy, it also will help fuel your drive to work hard. And seeing the fruits of your labor and the increase in profit becomes even more fulfilling than paying down debt, paying off your car, or building a nest egg.

Here are a few things to keep in mind:

Choose wisely. Don't give money away foolishly or to just anyone without due diligence. Take the time to think about the kind of organizations or causes you would like to support. Make sure they are near and dear to your heart and are using their finances ethically and in line with their mission.

Everywhere you turn, it seems someone is asking for money. Though many of these requests are for good causes, don't just give because you feel guilty. Give because you feel compassion for or closely connected to the particular cause, individual, or charity.

As we get solicitations for donations multiple times per week, my husband, Jesse, and I have a policy that we rarely give money to anyone we don't know personally or don't have some personal connection to. This might sound harsh to some of you, but doing so actually frees us up to research organizations we are specifically passionate about. This propels us to find that single mom who is working hard to make ends meet and write her an anonymous check, or find that family who needs a new furnace for winter and buy it for them, or help pay the mortgage payment for a neighbor who unexpectedly lost his job.

Our philosophy is to come alongside those who are working really hard and can't seem to catch a break and help give them a leg up. I have no desire—nor do I think it's wise for anyone—to give to those folks who just want an easy handout.

Stick with organizations and causes for a lengthy period of time. As our business has grown, we have loved finding a few organizations to partner with on a long-term basis. While we still give here and there for onetime causes, we prefer to have the bulk of our giving directed toward an ongoing stream. Not only does this method reap a big impact over time, it also allows us to build a longstanding relationship with the particular organization.

Consider setting up a recurring gift. If you don't have a lot of margin in your budget for charitable giving, there are many organizations that would welcome a small dollar amount on a consistent basis. For instance, you can sponsor a child through Compassion International for just forty dollars per month. Or, you can become a monthly sponsor of Mercy House Kenya (an organization I love!) for as low as ten dollars per month.

Keep receipts. Depending on where you give your dollars, you may be entitled to tax deductions or write-offs for charitable donations. I recommend speaking with an accountant or tax professional to ask for details on how to track your giving.

Ideas to Donate Your Dollars

Margaret commented on a blog post how blessed she feels with all that she has, even though it isn't much. She is inspired to give to others because she realizes how many people in this world go without the basics, like food and proper medical care. Margaret doesn't have thousands of dollars in her savings account, a six-figure salary, or a paid-off house. She supports her family on a single salary and has her share of debt that she's trying to pay off, but she still is intentional about leaving a mark. Just recently, she finished fully funding a microloan for a couple who is raising a grandchild after the death of their daughter. Although that required some tweaking in her own budget, Margaret was happy to help these people as she has raised her own grandson and understands the sacrifices that come with the responsibility.

Being involved in giving reminds us of what's really important. Below are some ideas on how you can use your money, however much or little, to make a difference:

- Support a local charity.
- Pay for a babysitter for a single mom or married couple who need a break.
- Buy grocery gift cards for a family experiencing a financial rough patch.
- Leave an extra tip for a server struggling to make ends meet.
- Donate food or toiletries to a local homeless shelter.
- Sponsor a child through Compassion International for around forty dollars per month.
- Put together bags with necessities (such as soap, socks, granola bars, toothpaste, and so on) and keep them in your glove compartment to hand out to homeless people.
- Call your local pregnancy crisis center or halfway house and ask what their greatest needs are and contribute toward or fill one.
- Visit your local hospital and bring bags with practical items such as toothpaste, deodorant, gift cards, and change for the vending machine, and pass them out to families who are there with a loved one.
- Donate food to your local food pantry, which is typically in need of healthy staple items.
- Anonymously leave a bag of groceries on someone's doorstep.
- Donate gently used outgrown clothes.
- Invite someone you know who has had a particularly rough couple of months out for coffee, a movie, or dinner. Sometimes people just want a chance to feel "normal."

Another practical way to live generously is to support companies and individuals who give. For instance, for years we used a large corporate web hosting service. It worked well for a season, but about two years ago we started having a lot of frustrating technical issues with our site. Because our hosting service employed thousands of people, the process of submitting a ticket through the help desk and waiting for someone to get back to us and resolve the issue took an incredibly long time, often through the course of many hours and involving multiple techs on different shifts. To say the least, these experiences left us feeling exasperated and having wasted much time.

In considering other options, my manager recommended someone he knew who had experience with large sites but worked for himself. After speaking with Mark, we decided he was a perfect fit for hosting our business. We've loved working with him. Not only is it such a relief to have direct, immediate, and personal help when issues arise, I love the fact that Mark employs a man in India who takes care of issues that come up in the middle of the night. What Mark pays this man helps not only support his immediate family but much of his extended family as well.

Now, when I need to hire someone for a short-term project or long-term position, I love to work with companies or contractors committed to giving and making a change in our culture. I always get so excited when I'm researching hiring potential companies or contractors and I read on their sites that they are committed to giving back in some way!

Living Generously on a Budget

When I was in the early years of blogging, my blogging friend Shannon Lowe (from *RocksInMyDryer.typepad.com*) went to Uganda with Compassion International (CI). Her mission was to live-blog about the child advocacy orchestrated by CI in that part of the world. I followed along with her journey through her website and was forever changed. My husband was unemployed at the time, and we were really struggling financially. But after reading her posts, we realized how much we truly had. I remember how humbled I was when I read Shannon's description of the living conditions of the village she visited.

The slums were just exactly like every picture you've seen of African urban poverty. The children ran around in rags, while adults sat outside their doors, many trying to sell things, others begging. Raw sewage ran in various open channels through the streets. Cows and chickens roamed freely, and the open-air market sold raw fish absolutely covered in flies. It is just exactly like I pictured a hundred times, just exactly like I'd seen in countless photos of Africa. And yet it was profoundly different, standing there, seeing it, smelling it, holding the hands of the children.

Our family had plenty to eat, access to clean water, clothes to wear, a roof over our heads, and indoor plumbing, to name a few "luxuries." While it seemed like money was tight for us, we didn't really know the first thing about poverty. So even though we had little wiggle room in our budget, we committed to sponsor two children through Compassion International. Until our income increased, we gave up our small "Eating Out" budget for a few months to come up with the funds. Compared to the circumstances these people in Uganda were living in, it was the least we could do.

You know what? We've been so blessed to step out and give, even when it meant some small sacrifices on our part. And we've learned that the more you freely and generously give, the more you receive—not necessarily always in the form of financial blessings, but in many other ways. Truly, it is "more blessed to give than to receive."[2]

One of the most exciting things about the growth of my blog is that it has given us more resources to be able to give. We've been able to help fund adoptions through Show Hope, help readers out in practical ways, fund a child survival program in the Dominican Republic through Compassion International, and help fund the operational expenses and pay for special projects in needy communities in South Africa. It gives me goose bumps to think that God is using this blog to feed and clothe the needy!

I know plenty of people who live on strict budgets and have significantly streamlined their spending habits but still intentionally reach out to their local community to show love, or to help someone who just lost his or her job, or to care for an ailing neighbor.

We all can do something. And our combined generosity can make a powerful difference—in the lives of those in our own community and in far-away countries!

It doesn't take much. Really, it doesn't. Don't feel incapable of living generously just because you don't have an extra hundred dollars or more to donate. I want you to feel hopeful because of the things you *are* able to do. And trust me on this one—there are a ton of things you can do! If you feel stretched to the max, here are some ways to make an impact on a limited income and for free:

- Donate books to your local library, schools, or members in your community.
- If you are a coupon queen and have built a stockpile of toiletries, household products, or cleaning items, donate them to a family in need in your neighborhood or to a local shelter.

- Buy handmade items made by entrepreneurs in third world countries. For instance, HeavenlyTreasures.org's mission is to equip and assist people in developing countries to break the cycle of poverty through their handiwork and creativity. This organization focuses on handicraft projects that allow the development of a micro enterprise, leading these folks down the path to self-sufficiency.
- Buy items you need, like shoes, from companies that give back. For example, for every shoe purchase you make, TOMS shoes gives a pair to a child in need.
- Volunteer. So many of my blog readers tell me about the opportunities they have to serve in their local soup kitchen, hospital, church, school, or charitable organization. Visit VolunteerMatch.org for an opportunity near you.
- Shop sales and clearance racks for significantly marked down merchandise you can donate to local families or organizations.
- Be socially responsible. Make it a priority to recycle, reuse resources (paper, technology, supplies), conserve energy, and minimize waste. Purchase services and products from ethically responsible and environmentally minded companies.
- Pick up prescriptions for elderly neighbors or ask them if they need someone to drive them to doctor's appointment or help with errands.
- Mow the lawn or weed the yard of a neighbor working multiple jobs.
- Supply freezer meals to a mother who just had a baby, a family who lost a loved one, or a neighbor who is sick.

- Donate your talents. If your hobby is photography, offer a financially struggling family a photo shoot. If you have a passion to sew or knit, make sweaters or scarves for a local shelter or hospital.
- Clean the house or do laundry for someone who is sick.

Investing Beyond Our Wallets and Closer to Home

Some of us get so focused on turning our attention and efforts toward helping others who are communities or oceans away that we miss opportunities presented right in front of our eyes. I want to talk about some practical, life-giving ways to make an impact closer to home.

William Arthur Ward said, "Do more than belong: participate. Do more than care: help. Do more than believe: practice. Do more than be fair: be kind. Do more than forgive: forget."[3] You can make a great impact simply by investing in those you have contact with regularly, whether family, friends, loved ones, clients, customers, or neighbors. When you extend kindness, grace, and compassion, you create a ripple effect that reaps lasting results.

I'll admit, sometimes doing this can be hard, especially in business when people are upset over something that you can't control, or when they are truly over-reacting, or when they blame you for a problem that is not your fault. However, I've found that not reacting in the same negative manner and instead responding in grace and remedying their problem with patience produces some incredible results.

When we first launched our downloadable grocery savings course called Grocery University, we ran a huge sale offering a steep discount. Thousands of products were sold in a short amount of time and, as is to be expected with any promotion of this size, we experienced some glitches and hiccups along the way. In addition, during a thirty-minute period of the sale, the online payment processing system went down. As a result, we received a few dozen e-mails from customers who were having trouble with their downloads or the payment process. A few didn't hesitate to spew their feelings of anger and frustration, saying all sorts of crazy things in caps! Well, I told my team that we would provide to whoever had trouble with their purchase a free download as well as refund money to those who had already paid and continued to experience technical problems. It was amazing to see how quickly the attitudes of those few irate customers changed from our response. Many were grateful and gracious—and some even apologetic for their outbursts—in turn.

There are many ways—great and small—to invest in others. Before I talk about building and nurturing relationships with your friends and loved ones, I want to shine a practical spotlight on what you can do today that will make an immediate difference in your business:

- Go the extra mile for a customer.
- Care about people: ask how they are doing, listen to their answers, and show interest.
- Be respectful, fair, and ethical in dealing with vendors.
- Show appreciation to your clients by sending them a handwritten note (takes more effort than an e-mail) or small gift.
- Be especially patient when dealing with an unsatisfied or irate client or customer. Consider that person's point of view.
- Mentor, coach, or share valuable knowledge with others. If someone is just starting out in his or her business, help that person along the way by providing insight you've learned.

One simple thing that I've done is to take time to pray for people. When I read an e-mail or comment from blog readers who are having a rough time, I try to stop what I'm doing and take a moment to pray for them, letting them know afterward that I thought of them and what I've specifically prayed. I've been amazed at how much this little act of kindness means to people. It also allows me to be present with others instead of being inundated with just my own little world.

Invest in Others

For years, I didn't have many close friends. I had handfuls of acquaintances but very few people with whom I could be completely honest.

I was insecure and a people-pleaser, so I always held back in relationships. I didn't want to say the wrong thing or come across in the wrong way. Because of this, I usually didn't share things I was thinking about, working through, or struggling with at a deep level.

While this allowed me to not get so hurt in relationships and kept me more "safe," it also meant that I felt lonely much of the time. I wanted to have intimate friendships, but I was scared of opening up and being vulnerable.

My personal journey from insecurity to confidence has transformed me from the inside out. And it has also given me courage to step outside of the safe zone and reach out to people around me in an authentic way.

It's taken years to get to this place, but I am so blessed to now have a group of really close friends. Friends who would drop everything to help me. Friends who I can share anything with and they will listen and won't think I'm crazy (or maybe they think I'm crazy sometimes, but they still love me!). Friends who are life-giving. Friends who love me enough to have earned the right to speak the truth to me when I need to hear it. Friends who I just love hanging out with and sharing life with.

It's important to invest in quality relationships while life and your blossoming business spin in furious circles. You cannot isolate yourself behind the curtain of your laptop, growth goals, financial ambitions, or marketing strategies. No man is an island, right?

Spending quality time with your friends and family is a surefire way to encourage you and fuel your productivity. It will keep you from feeling drained, tired, and discouraged. So make an effort to invest in people around you—your spouse, your children, your parents, your siblings, your neighbors, your friends.

Here are some ways to foster relationships:

- Take time to listen, even when your elderly neighbor drones on and on sharing the same story she told you last week.
- Send your spouse a text message in the middle of the day to say "I love you."
- Write a note of encouragement to a friend who is going through a tough time.
- Pray for your sister—and let her know you did.
- Send a care package of goodies to a friend who struggles with depression.

Whether you are playing dolls with your daughter, chatting over coffee with a best friend, or cooking dinner with a neighbor, be present. Look into that person's eyes. Listen. Really listen. Ask good questions. Focusing fully on another person without being distracted by e-mail or Facebook shows you truly care—and makes a huge difference.

Sacrifices and Blessings

Some time ago, I was excited to get a great deal on an item we needed. After I bought it, God strongly prompted me to give the item to a friend who is going through a difficult financial situation.

I struggled to follow the prompting as I knew this was an item we needed, and I wasn't sure if I'd be able to find a good deal on it again for a while. But I willingly gave it to my friend because I just knew in my heart that was what I was supposed to do.

There was so much joy in doing this. And I realized that I could always pay full-price if I had to because following what God called me to do was more important than saving money. In the meantime, I knew we could live a little while without the item, so I figured I would hold off as long as I could and see if another great deal came along.

Well, not two days later, an acquaintance e-mailed me out of the blue and said she had a package they wanted to send to me and could I please e-mail her my new address? Can you guess what arrived in that package yesterday? The exact same item I had given to my friend—only this was a bigger and better version.

In recent years, God has been teaching me that it can be easy to give from our abundance, but true giving requires sacrifice. Living generously doesn't necessarily mean feeling good about yourself just because you handed twenty bucks to some homeless man on the street. Or just because you gave something away.

Since I'm not very attached to stuff, giving away items to other people is fun but relatively easy to do. For instance, if I'm going to get rid of some old clothes or furniture, is it really a sacrifice to pass it on to a friend instead of tossing it in the Goodwill box? No, not really.

Giving of my time and effort, on the other hand, is an area where

I often struggle. I can be stingy when it comes to setting aside my neatly planned-out day to meet a need in someone's life.

When a child needs me to drop everything I'm doing to help him or her with something, I can feel frustrated that I've been needlessly interrupted. Or when my husband calls and asks me to run an errand for him, my natural reaction is to feel irritated.

For me, that's often the giving that matters the most. Because it's giving where it really costs something.

I've found that every time I give in a way that requires sacrifice, I'm so very blessed in the end. And it inspires me to let go even more and live with arms stretched out wide.

When Maria thinks about the blessings involved with sacrifice, her dad quickly comes to mind. He owns a hardware/auto supply store in the Philippines and understands how important it is to support those less fortunate. Maria's dad plants rice not only for his family's sustenance but he also donates a portion of his crops to the local parish seminary and the poor in his community. A humble man, he is admired by many for his compassion and giving spirit.

A few years back, a fire broke out in the area where his store is located. Helpless, this man watched as the buildings and houses that surrounded his shop lit up in roaring flames, many quickly disintegrating before his eyes in an unrecognizable pile of ashes. As the fire loomed closer to his business, threatening to destroy the shop in mere minutes, something immediately caught his eye. Maria's father saw a line of people, the very men and women he had fed and served in town, passing buckets of sloshing water to one another to help douse the flames. By nothing short of a miracle and the courageous acts of many, the fire was contained. The man's shop stood, unscathed by flames.

Maria's dad was grateful beyond words, and as best as he could, he conveyed his appreciation to those selfless men and women. One person clapped him on the back and told him she simply would not have allowed the store to burn down because of how much he has done for others. Wow! I can't help but tear up as I share this story.

The value that your life can provide to others and the impact you can make on others' lives is phenomenal—even if it seems as though you don't have a lot to offer. Sara is a blogger who over the years has grown a decent-sized platform, which brings in some income. She uses this money to pay for her family's groceries and extras while the income from her husband's business, though irregular, pays for all other expenses.

As a mom of a child with special needs, Sara's heart is bent toward orphans with disabilities. A year ago, when her household income was barely enough to pay the bills, she had a deep desire to donate her entire blog earnings to a special needs adoption advocacy group. It was quite a financial sacrifice, especially considering her husband's business at the time was slow.

Prior to making a final decision, a fellow entrepreneur gave Sara advice she never forgot: "God will take care of your business when you keep His business (helping others) a priority." When Sara thought about the vast needs around the world—from hunger to homelessness to disease to abandoned orphans—she realized she was blessed far more than she wanted to admit. So she took the plunge. Here is what Sara has to say:

So while going into our slowest period of the year, in which I saw our own pantry supplies dwindling, we decided that any income through my blog would go straight into the adoption fund for a waiting special needs child. The result? Not only was I able to raise double my goal, and in record time, a certain little boy with Down syndrome who had lived without the love of a family his whole life finally found his Forever Family! And not once did our family go hungry! Yes, we had to say no to our children when they asked for special treats or toys, but when we realized the impact our family had, the sacrifice was worth it all!

Living generously in this way has sparked a lifestyle of benevolence that has poured itself into her husband's business. The company now helps support various missions and charities as Sara continues to contribute blog revenue toward special needs adoption and other children in need.

One of our greatest desires should be to live willingly and gladly giving of our best for others. Holding nothing back. And when our days come to a close, we should be able to say without regret that we used everything we were given—for others. For your family, your friends, strangers in need, struggling neighbors, and even for those we may never meet in this lifetime. That's how we truly live with a generous spirit.

Here's to Your Success!

Begin, be bold, and venture to be wise.

—HORACE

SO HERE YOU ARE. PERHAPS YOU HAVE ALREADY BEGUN TO unfold your unique plan to earn income, whether to support your family, meet certain financial goals, or build a bigger cushion to help those who may be without.

And I hope that through these pages and the marvelous stories of the many women I have been blessed to meet . . .

Your creativity has been sparked.

Your heart stirred.

Vision birthed.

Ideas born.

I want to tell you how proud I am that you have taken ownership of your finances, your dreams, your strategies, and your future. From the bottom of my heart, I truly commend and applaud you.

Through these pages, together we have walked through the practices, practicalities, and possibilities of increasing your income. You've learned how to do the following:

- Unleash the power of financial freedom to begin to live on less and be in a position to help others.
- Discover your unique skills, talents, passions, and knowledge that, coupled with an existing need in a market, can provide an avenue to generate income.
- Take appropriate steps to research, learn, and understand the best business to build and sustain, even when the going gets tough (and it will!).
- Pinpoint the why of your business or idea so you effectively tailor your offered services or products, branding, marketing, and other business needs.
- Expand your thinking to consider earning residual income and a slew of other clever money-making ideas you may want to adopt.
- Tackle slow, steady, and successful growth as your business expands financially and with manpower.
- Conquer saboteurs that stand in your way, including insecurity, fear of failure, lack of time, and healthy work-life balance.
- Reshift your perspective on life and money to begin living generously for others.

- Intentionalize giving through myriad channels, whether financial, through your time, your attention, or by being present with those closest to you.

As I begin this final chapter of the book, I want to talk about expectations. I can't tell you how quickly you are going to start making money or how much. I can't tell you exactly what challenge you will face with your particular idea. Nor can I give you a step-by-step plan to growing your particular business within however many months you want it to grow.

Stay with me.

What I can tell you is to count on some detours—plans that may not work out, a contract that may not go through, a deadline that may not be met, a sale that does not happen—you know, setbacks.

Expect Change . . . and Know What to Do About It

While it's always wise to be strategic and head into any venture with a long-term plan, understand that plans may change because, well, life changes. Circumstances change. And so do opportunities. Setbacks in business are a reality. Maybe your advertisements have not brought in as many clients as you expected. Perhaps you find your market saturated with similar products to yours. Or maybe you discover that another contractor landed that coveted job instead of you.

Not too long ago, I got an e-mail from a reader who works full-time and desperately wants to start her own business, but she just keeps hitting brick walls. Days earlier, she was excited because she had an interview scheduled with a virtual assistant company and was confident she had a good chance at the position. While she prepared as best as she could and stayed optimistic, she didn't end up getting the job. She was devastated, discouraged, and disheartened. She longs to have less of a commute, to be home more, and to be less tied down to a job, but so far, every time she's tried to find a work-at-home job, she's been met instead with a slammed door in her face. She feels completely stuck.

Maybe you can relate.

Another friend of mine had been working really hard to grow his online business and experienced great results. But in the past few months, progress has slowed considerably. In fact, the pace of his business is at a standstill or even dropping off. My friend is frustrated because he invested much time and effort for what feels like nothing.

I can relate to him in many ways, because right before I began working on this book, I had a major setback in my business. For months, my Facebook page had been growing like crazy—to the tune of thousands of new followers every single week! I had experimented with a lot of different things and finally found a system for how and when to post. This strategy worked incredibly well and kept engagement and click-throughs at an all-time high.

For months, the payoff was great. In 2013, our Facebook followers grew by over two hundred thousand followers, our traffic numbers to my website doubled, and our unique visitors almost doubled. The growth was phenomenal and best of all, organic; we didn't spend a dime advertising on Facebook. And then, about a year later, we had a Facebook post go viral unlike anything we'd ever experienced before. It was insane—millions and millions of people saw the post, hundreds of thousands of people liked and shared the post, our Facebook page follower numbers grew to over six hundred thousand, and our already-massive Facebook engagement blew up even more. I was so excited! We'd set some pretty audacious goals for 2014 and this was going to help us skyrocket and hit those goals much more quickly than I had expected.

But about five days later, something weird happened. It was as if Facebook decided not to show any of my posts to anyone because of the one post that had gone viral. I'm not kidding. Whereas in the past my posts were shown to at least 30 percent (and often 50 percent) of our hundreds of thousands of followers, now only 1 to 3 percent of our followers were being shown my posts.

Comments and likes that had once poured in now trickled into a few here, a few there. Traffic dropped significantly. And our income took a nosedive.

For weeks, we tried everything under the sun I could come up with, but nothing fixed the problem. I was at my wit's end. I'd never experienced something as unusual as this before. Whenever we'd hit a hiccup with Facebook in the past, after a few days of experimenting, I could figure out how to tweak our posting methods so that we'd be back to normal—or even better.

But this time, none of our hoped-for solutions made a difference. I researched. I prayed. I talked to other Facebook page owners. I researched some more, prayed some more, and by this time felt like pulling my hair out.

We had depended so heavily on Facebook for traffic that when the bottom fell out, every part of our business was hurt—traffic, income, engagement, and the ability to help people through the information we offered on our posts. I worried about what it would mean long-term if things didn't pick back up again. I had just taken on a lot of new expenses, including upgrading our monthly website hosting and hiring some new team members. *Would we continue to turn a profit?*

I felt frustrated, and my family couldn't help but notice and be affected by my high stress level. I couldn't relax. I couldn't have fun. And I couldn't fully enjoy life, or my family, because I was constantly analyzing what I could do to improve Facebook and stressing over how we were going to weather this over the long haul. I was snappy, sleep-deprived, and grumpy.

I finally realized that all of this worry and frustration was accomplishing nothing good. I had done everything I could do to fix the problem, and it was time to step back and reevaluate Facebook, the business as a whole, and how I was going to pick back up and start afresh.

Here are three actions I took that enabled me to rebound from my setback—not only giving me a lot more peace but also helping me to have renewed passion and purpose.

Revisit the Why

This dip in traffic and Facebook engagement caused me to realize that some of my enthusiasm and fulfillment was being fueled by numbers, not purely by passion.

I had to stop and reevaluate the why behind what I'm doing. I spent time mulling over all the reasons I started MoneySavingMom .com in the first place. It wasn't so I could build a large platform or have a thriving Facebook page (Facebook pages didn't even exist when I started!).

My why was to help people find practical ways to save money so they can experience the freedom and blessings that come from living with intention.

Reminding myself of this mission has really changed my perspective, renewed my enthusiasm, and given me a burning drive to continue on. It also resurrected some of the types of posts and series that I used to write when the blog was still in its early stages. I wanted to talk about everyday life stuff—posts where I shared my thoughts, the lessons I was learning, and the things our family was doing. Posts that offered a peek into our home and family life. Posts that were straight from my heart, raw and unedited.

Honestly, I was scared to go back to old-fashioned blogging. The Internet had evolved so much since I'd started. Everything was more beautiful and professional—you know, Pinterest-perfect. I didn't know what my readers would think or if they would even stick around if I started sharing a lot more journal-entry-type posts with pictures and details of our everyday life. But I knew that's where my heart was, so I wrote an entry explaining why I was making the shift and then jumped in with both feet.

The response blew me away. My readers were so supportive, it was clear they were hungry for more real-life stuff. They've been interacting with one another more than ever through comments, and I've received more e-mails and notes than I can count from readers thanking me for the change. This would not have happened had it not been for my Facebook page tanking. And it has renewed my enthusiasm for blogging and my readers' enthusiasm for reading!

Not too long ago, I was sitting next to a writer at an afternoon tea event. She shared with me about the book she planned on writing and allowed me to have a peek at her outline. I thought her idea was brilliant and much needed. As she expressed deep enthusiasm for the project, I interrupted her and said, "You know this excitement and passion you feel for this project right now? You know how you feel like this topic is so necessary to write about? You know how you are telling me all the ways this book is going to benefit others? I want you to remember this moment. I want you to remember this passion and enthusiasm and vision and purpose you have. Because when you get into the thick of writing this book, there will be many moments when it will be hard. It will require sacrifice and struggle. If you don't continually go back to your why when the going gets tough, you're going to lose your spark and burn out before the project is completed. Let this passion fuel your writing."

What's your why? To help financially support your family? To teach people how to become more organized? To bring hope to those who are struggling? To help support the widow down the street? To help pay off your daughter's medical bills from her recent surgery? To help pay off your family's credit card bills? To contribute toward your community youth center? Whatever your reason(s) for earning money, remember why you're doing it. Always keep the vision before your eyes.

Remember the Progress

Setbacks can discourage and dishearten us if we focus on how far we are from where we'd hoped to be. I spent weeks carrying around discouragement over this Facebook situation. But then I finally woke up and realized how unproductive this was. And truth be told, a few years ago, I would have been thrilled to be where we are right now business-wise. It's far beyond what I could have ever dreamed or imagined.

When I stopped feeling exasperated and, instead, looked at the enormous blessings, I was able to see many incredible things to be grateful for. And this really encouraged and excited me!

Just today, I got an e-mail from a fellow blogger who was discouraged because she had received notice from Amazon saying they were only going to be able to pay her a fourth of what they'd been paying her for promoting their deals on her site. Right now, the majority of her blogging income is from affiliate revenue from Amazon, so getting her earnings so drastically cut came as quite a shock. She didn't know what she was going to do. Since Amazon has done the same thing to me—they had cut my affiliate fees from 8 percent to .8 percent—I knew how frustrated she felt. It's a crushing blow to see your hard-earned effort slip through your fingers, and it feels like there's nothing you can do about it.

Gratefully, I was able to share with her how my Facebook setback propelled me to think outside the box. And in changing my strategy and shifting my efforts in a few different areas, we have slowly been bringing our traffic numbers back up. They aren't where they were, but I'm so encouraged by the continued upward trend. Talking to this blogger reminded me of how far I've come. Now, instead of feeling down about Facebook numbers, I felt encouraged, hope-filled, and excited about what I've learned from the experience.

Don't allow a slip of your footing to bring you totally down. Use the experience to inspire you to think creatively and motivate you to rethink your options and strategies. When you do this, you make progress. And when you focus on the steps or leaps of change you make, you subtract attention and time away from your setback and instead continue your forward momentum.

Rethink the Expectations

Because of the changes with Facebook, I have to change my expectations and projections and goals. This is not failing; this is being realistic.

I need to stop comparing things to what they once were and start creating new goals and projections based upon where things are right now. Otherwise, I'm going to feel overwhelmed, constantly behind, and like I'm perpetually failing.

Taking the unrealistic expectations off my shoulders gave me massive relief. And it has allowed me to start celebrating the small wins again!

Don't expect overnight success. Expect slow and steady growth.

Don't expect every idea or every strategy to triumph every time. Expect failure to be a part of the learning process.

Don't expect that you'll never run into personnel issues or clients who are upset. Expect that you'll have difficult situations and will need to show grace.

Don't expect that you know everything about running a business. Expect that there are going to be massive learning curves and struggles along the way.

Don't expect what worked yesterday to work in three months. Expect to experiment and learn as your variables around your business change.

The Final Send-Off

As your excitement builds at the potential financial freedom offers and as you may be brainstorming a particular idea, working through details of a possible business, or already celebrating your first client, I want to leave you with three keys.

Be Consistent

I think one of the greatest markers of success is consistency. If you're a blogger, this means regularly posting great content and corresponding with your readers. If you own a storefront business, this means opening the doors on time and offering quality products. If you're a consultant for an accounting firm, it means producing superior work with each contract. If readers, consumers, clients, or customers know they can count on you, they are much more likely to regularly show up and use your services or products.

Whatever you choose to do, take your job seriously. Keep your commitments. Treat your business just like you'd treat your job if you were working for someone else. Because you are working for someone else: your customers!

Someone asked me not too long ago what the secret was to my success. My answer: "There are no secrets; just hard work." I have blogged almost every single day but Sunday, every single week, every single year since I began blogging in 2005.

That's a lot of blogging. And trust me, while I truly love it, there were days when I would have rather been doing something else—catching up on sleep, for one. I have stayed up late at night, gotten up early in the morning, and worked on Saturdays and holidays. There have been grueling and exhausting seasons, but the commitment, drive, and consistency have paid off in big ways.

This book is scheduled to release ten years after I first started my own business. I look back on those years and realize that where I am today is not anywhere near where I expected I would be. I thought I'd probably always have some kind of side business, but I never would have imagined running a full-time business, making more than a full-time income, and having sixteen people on my team!

It's fascinating to look back and see how law school—what we thought would be the catalyst for my husband to start a success-ful career—ended up being a stepping-stone for a much bigger ministry and business than we could have ever dreamed. The lessons we learned during those lean law school years allowed us to teach hundreds of thousands of families around the globe how to cut their grocery bills and get their finances in order. The struggles we endured financially allowed us to be much more compassionate and empathetic with those who are barely getting by. The experience we gained at sticking with a budget when things were tighter than tight allowed us to be able to inspire other people to live with intention when it comes to finances. The contentment that we gleaned from those years when we didn't have any extra wiggle room has allowed us to continue to live on little, even as our income has significantly increased. It's amazing what's possible when you consistently show up, do the work, and stay the course.

Stay Focused

If you want to get things done, stop doing a hundred things at once. Yes, I know, right now you might be feeling overwhelmed with your business ideas list and your business to-do list. You want to finish your website, start blogging, set up meetings with three potential customers, look for networking events in your area, research advertising options, read those three business books, and look into licensing laws for your state.

Your brain is swimming with ideas, but you're also in the middle of all the real-life, everyday stuff—like buying a dress for your sister's wedding, baking a cake for your son's birthday party, getting the mountain of dishes done, taking the dog to the vet, visiting your mother, and writing overdue thank-you notes.

Multi-tasking can seem like a very efficient strategy to knock out our to-dos one by one. And while studies have shown that women are hardwired to be better at doing this compared to men, it doesn't necessarily mean we can do it all and do it well. In fact, juggling multiple tasks simultaneously can lead to distractions, which can result in getting nothing done.

In order to accomplish concentrated work in an efficient manner, create a distraction-free zone. Shut out the noise and focus on one thing at a time. Set a particular time frame around your tasks, whether it's twenty minutes or one hour.

If it's time to e-mail, e-mail. Go through your e-mails in order of priority and don't stop until your time is up. If it's time to research something, do only research. If you need to make a phone call, just make the phone call.

If you're used to working on your computer while you have a bunch of applications open and with your phone constantly dinging, you'll be surprised at how much work you can get done in a distraction-free, twenty-to thirty-minute concentrated block of time.

And once you get in the habit of doing one thing at a time, you'll find your fizzle point, the time your energy wanes and you need to stop what you're doing and take a break so you can return to your project refreshed and reignited. Personally, I've found that I do best by working in twenty-to thirty-minute blocks and then rewarding myself with a short five-minute break to check e-mail or read something online. If I'm working on an in-depth project that requires a lot of brainpower, I'll often set a timer for twenty minutes and work on it and then set the timer for a fifteen-minute break to clean or play with the kids.

Remember What Matters

Knowing the basics of earning money is a good thing. It's smart. It's wise to invest in your present and future by building a foundation for financial freedom. But if you research, analyze, gather ideas, collect information, implement strategies, build products, or hone your skills without a vision of impacting others, value will be lost. Your efforts will lack some meaning. You'll get that twitch in your spirit every now and again of feeling empty, like something is missing.

I want to leave you with two stories that I recently read that have reminded me of the power of influence we have.

Kristen, one of my blog readers, e-mailed to tell me about her friend Lal, who is a small-business owner in Kansas City. Six years ago, Lal and her family came to the States as refugees and opened an Asian grocery store to serve the growing population of refugees from Burma. Lal's real passion is supporting the youth in her community and feels that her store is a tool to do so. She understands that young refugees coming to this country are vulnerable to negative influences while trying to fit in and integrate into society.

Lal knew the first step to being able to make a big impact was to expand her store and open a restaurant. She did this the second year in operation with the goal of having more profits to pour into a youth ministry. This summer, just five months after moving to a new location and starting construction on the kitchen, Lal launched Galilee Youth Ministry in collaboration with several young leaders in the Burmese Chin community. She held a nine-week program for kids that included language classes, a meal each day, spiritual instruction, and transportation—all offered at no cost.

Kristen helped Lal in this venture and was taken aback by her friend's passionate vision and faith. She says,

Unlike Lal, I am not an entrepreneur, so as we planned for the summer I kept seeing "logical" administrative-type reasons of why we shouldn't start (there weren't enough teachers, we didn't have a curriculum, and so on), but Lal didn't give up. She stayed faithful to the vision God gave her and served over 50 children.

This is powerful stuff! Understanding her business was a conduit to make a difference, Lal pushed forward, actualized growth, and brought opportunities to young people they wouldn't have had otherwise.

Impacting others isn't a one-size-fits-all deal. It doesn't matter if you contribute your time, your resources, or your money; helping others in any way is the heartbeat of living generously.

Pruett is a single mother of two children. Her youngest has special needs and is also a type 1 diabetic. Holidays are rough and though this mom can't always give her children everything she'd like, they are loved, taken care of, and have everything they need. When her now-teenage son was in kindergarten, Pruett was saddened by the high number of kids in the school district who lived in poverty. Knowing many of them wouldn't receive anything for Christmas, she surprised some of them with presents and continued this tradition for several years.

Sometime later, through a program with a local group home, Pruett "adopted" two teenage boys without family who lived there. When Christmas rolled around, these boys asked for everyday items like coats, hats, and underwear. Pruett was shocked that a child would even consider these things to be a "gift."

She decided, along with her children, to get these boys everything they asked for. It meant she had to use most of her Christmas budget on children she would likely never meet. And it meant her own family had to make sacrifices, but they all were happy to do this. Pruett bought and wrapped the gifts, and a volunteer at the group home picked up the presents at her workplace.

A few weeks later Pruett was transitioning into a new job that was closer to home and offered a better salary. On the last day of work at her old job, security notified her that there was a package for her at the front desk. Pruett told me:

I assumed it was a package of paperwork to fill out for my exit interview. I picked it up and didn't think much of it for the rest of the day. When I got home I remembered that package in my bag. To my utter shock it wasn't paperwork at all. It was a framed picture of the Christmas tree at the group home with the packages we'd sent underneath it. All of the boys at the home had signed the picture. That picture is still on my bureau after all this time. I look at it every day and think about those boys. That Christmas was so much more than just wrapping up socks and hats for children I'll never know. I am blessed every day to know that I made a difference in their lives.

Remember, friend, you are an instrument of blessing. You were made for a purpose. You have unique gifts, skills, knowledge, passions, and experience.

Use the ideas and practical tools presented in the pages of this book to chart a course for success. Always remember that money is first and foremost a tool—something that can not only bring more financial peace and stability into your home but that can make a big difference in your community and around the world.

Keep dreaming, keep setting goals, and keep breaking them down into bite-size pieces. Keep moving forward, even if you feel like you're going at a snail's pace.

Don't give up. Don't buy into the belief that says you don't have anything to offer.

You are the only you in existence. The world needs your story. The world needs your gifts. The world needs you.

May your life be a force that channels change in this world.

The Money-Making Mom Manifesto is a summary of the important points in this book. As a business owner, it's easy to get bogged down in the urgent details of the day and forget your why. The Manifesto is a great way to help you keep the "most important things" top of mind. To download a FREE printable copy, please visit moneysavingmom.com/manifesto.

Money-Making Mom Manifesto

- I choose to make wise financial decisions and commit to building financial freedom for me (and my family).
- I choose to discover my skills, talents, passions, and knowledge and determine ways to translate them into an income-earning opportunity.
- I choose to consider whether starting my own business and working for myself is a viable option for my future.
- I choose to create a succinct vision for my business or idea and create a solid action plan I will implement.
- I choose to research and explore possibilities of earning income through residual growth, diversification, and other means.
- I choose to grow my business slowly and steadily and not hastily add expenses or employees until I can afford to do so.
- I choose to look beyond the paralyzing effects of fear and failure and press through my insecurities.
- I choose to commit to live generously, viewing my time, resources, and money as tools to be used for good.
- I choose to equate sacrifices with blessings, knowing however I can impact others will provide eternal value.

Resources

Websites

MakeOverYourMornings.com

MysteryShop.org

WAHM.com

BloggingWithAmy.com

MichaelHyatt.com

AmyPorterfield.com

MoneySavingMom.com/make-money-blogging

PlatformUniversity.com

CompelTraining.com

Books

The Bootstrap VA by Lisa Morosky

Eat That Frog: 21 Great Ways to Stop Procrastinating by Brian Tracy

EntreLeadership by Dave Ramsey

The Fringe Hours by Jessica Turner

How to Blog for Profit Without Selling Your Soul by Ruth Soukup

How to Have a 48-Hour Day by Don Aslett

The One Thing by Gary Keller

168 Hours: You Have More Time Than You Think by Laura Vanderkam

The Other 8 Hours by Robert Paglierini

Quitter by Jon Acuff

Say Goodbye to Survival Mode by Crystal Paine

Secrets of Dynamic Communication by Ken Davis

Sell Your Book Like Wildfire by Rob Eager

Start by Jon Acuff

Steal Like an Artist by Austin Kleon

Tell Your Time (ebook) by Amy Lynn Andrews

21 Days to a More Disciplined Life by Crystal Paine

What the Most Successful People Do Before Breakfast by Laura Vanderkam

What the Most Successful People Do on the Weekend by Laura Vanderkam

Podcasts

Brilliant Business Moms

Online Marketing Made Easy with Amy Porterfield

This Is Your Life with Michael Hyatt

Smart Passive Income with Pat Flynn

The Andy Stanley Leadership podcast

The Art and Business of Public Speaking

Notes

Chapter 3: The 8-to-5 Cure: Working for Yourself

1. "Babe Ruth – Quotes," *BabeRuth.com*, last modified 2011, accessed July 21, 2015, http://www.baberuth.com/quotes/.

Chapter 4: Get Moving, Start Building

1. P.J. Huffstutter, "How I Made It: Lizanne Falsetto, Founder of ThinkProducts," *Los Angeles Times*, March 27, 2011, accessed July 21, 2015, http://articles.latimes.com/2011/mar/27/business/la-fi-himi -thinkthin-20110327.
2. "Our business idea," *Ikea.com*, accessed July 21, 2015, http://www.ikea.com /ms/en_IE/about_ikea/the_ikea_way/our_business_idea/index.html.
3. "Harris Teeter, Inc.," *Company-Histories.com*, accessed July 21, 2015, http://www.company-histories.com/Harris-Teeter-Inc-Company-History .html.

Chapter 6: Growing Your Business

1. "Theodore Roosevelt Quotes," *TheodoreRooseveltCenter.org*, accessed July 21, 2015, http://www.theodorerooseveltcenter.org/Learn-About-TR /TR-Quotes.aspx.
2. "How I Made It: Lizanne Falsetto, founder of ThinkProducts," *Los Angeles Times*, March 27, 2011, http://articles.latimes.com/2011/mar/27 /business/la-fi-himi-thinkthin-20110327.

3. From a blog post on *JonAcuff.com*, accessed April 9, 2013 (site discontinued).

4. Rory Vaden featured on "Rabbi Daniel Lapin: Business Secrets from the Bible," February 9, 2015, accessed July 21, 2015, https://www.entre leadership.com/podcasts/rabbi-daniel-lapin-on-business-secrets-f.

Chapter 7: What Gets in the Way

1. "The Wizard's Wisdom: 'Woodenisms,'" *Espn.com*, June 5, 2010, accessed July 21, 2015, http://sports.espn.go.com/ncb/news/story?id=5249709.

2. Michael Hyatt, "Why Frequent Trips Outside Your Comfort Zone Are So Important," MichaelHyatt.com, August 6, 2012, accessed July 21, 2015, http://michaelhyatt.com/outside-your-comfort-zone.html.

Chapter 8: Live Generously

1. Clive Hamilton, *Growth Fetish* (London: Pluto Press, 2004), 213.

2. Samuel Johnson, The Rambler, March 24, 1750.

3. Shelene Bryan, *Love, Skip, Jump: Start Living the Adventure of Yes* (Nashville: Nelson Books, 2014), 65.

4. Erin Loury, "How to Become an Expert Tightrope Walker," *Science*, April 18, 2012, accessed July 21, 2015, http://news.sciencemag. org/2012/04/how-become-expert-tightrope-walker.

5. "How To Bloom Where You're Planted In 2014," *Forbes*, December 2, 2013, http://www.forbes.com/sites/robasghar/2013/12/02/how-to-bloom -where-youre-planted-in-2014/.

6. Ibid.

7. Shauna Niequist, *Bread and Wine: A Love Letter to Life Around the Table with Recipes* (Grand Rapids: Zondervan, 2013), 166.

8. Brendon Burchard, *The Charge* (New York: Free Press, 2012), 157.

9. Lisa-Jo Baker, "About Lisa-Jo Baker," *Lisajobaker.com*, accessed July 21, 2015, http://lisajobaker.com/about-lisa-jo-baker/.

10. Lisa-Jo Baker, "How to Get More Passion in Your Life," *Lisajobaker.com*, February 13, 2014, accessed July 21, 2015, http://lisajobaker.com/2014 /02/how-to-get-more-passion-in-your-life/.

Chapter 9: How to Give?

1. Leo Rosten, "On Finding Truth: Abandon the Strait Jacket of Conformity (Text of an address by Leo Rosten at the National Book Awards in New York)," April 8, 1962, The Sunday Star, Washington, DC, E-2.

2. Acts 20:35.
3. William Arthur Ward quoted in Mary Jo Ricketson, Moving Meditation: Experience the Good Within (Bloomington, IN: WestBow Press, 2011), 39.

About the Author

Crystal Paine is a child of God, wife, homeschool mom of three, businesswoman, author, and speaker. In 2007, she founded MoneySavingMom.com, a site that has grown to be one of the most popular blogs on the web, currently averaging close to 1.2 million readers per month. Her mission is to challenge women to manage their time and resources wisely and live life on purpose.

WANT TO MAKE A DIFFERENCE?

#TENDOLLARTRIBE

Earlier in this book I shared the story of Lisa-Jo and how she used the power of her blog to make a huge difference in South Africa.

In January of 2015, we went to South Africa together and my life was forever changed. I fell madly in love with both the beautiful country and the amazing people.

JOIN THE TEN DOLLAR TRIBE!

I'd like to invite you to join me in making a difference in South Africa by becoming a member of the Ten Dollar Tribe and committing to give $10 each month to support the work of Take Action Ministry and Help One Now in some of the poorest communities in South Africa.

Ten dollars might not seem like much, but it can make a major impact in South Africa. For instance, $10 will buy 100 bowls of porridge for school children, a month's worth of school supplies, or two weeks of cooking fuel for a local family.

If dozens of us are willing to take a step and make this commitment, it will impact the lives of hundreds of children for years to come.

Will you join us?

FIND OUT MORE AT **MoneySavingMom.com/Tribe**

Do you often wake up feeling behind before you even get out of bed?

Are you **forever frustrated** that it seems like you are so busy, but you have very little to show for all your effort?

Are you **worn down and worn out** by all the hats you are wearing and balls you are juggling?

Do you wish you could find time to **refuel your tank, improve your health, invest more into your family**, or even just to **slow down and breathe?**

You don't have to keep living life feeling constantly behind, overworked & overwhelmed!

Sign up today for Crystal's 14-day Make Over Your Mornings online course and learn how to **revolutionize your productivity, streamline your routines, invest your time in things that truly matter,** and **find more joy and peace** in the process.

MAKE OVER YOUR *mornings*

Find out more at MakeOverYourMornings.com